PLANT-BASED

COOKBOOK FOR BEGINNERS

2024

Delicious & Easy Vegan Recipes for a Healthy Lifestyle. Transform Your Diet with a 28-Day Meal Plan for Balanced Nutrition and Wellness.

Thea Mallin

Disclaimer
The information in this cookbook is for general informational purposes only. The author and publisher are not responsible for any adverse effects or consequences from the use of the recipes or information provided. Nutritional information is estimated and may vary. Consult a healthcare professional for personalized advice.

Published by THEA MALLIN

2024

Table of contents

INTRODUCTION

Greetings and welcome to the "Plant-Based Cookbook for Beginners" and your new culinary adventure! This book is your ticket to a tasty and nourishing lifestyle, whether your goal is to achieve better health, reduce environmental impact, or simply satisfy your curiosity. This eating style focuses on whole, minimally processed plant-based foods, offering a comprehensive approach to nutrition that goes beyond simple dietary decisions.

My quest for better health led me down the path of plant-based eating, which has since evolved into a passion for colorful, healthful food that feeds both the body and the soul. It all started a few years ago when I was struggling with fatigue and digestive issues. After countless doctor visits and various treatments, I decided to take control of my health by changing my diet. Inspired by documentaries and books about the benefits of plant-based eating, I made the leap and began experimenting with plant-based recipes.

Initially, the transition was challenging. I had to learn new cooking techniques and familiarize myself with a variety of new ingredients. However, as I delved deeper, I discovered a vibrant world of flavors and textures that I had never experienced before. The positive changes in my health were remarkable—I had more energy, improved digestion, and a renewed sense of well-being. This transformation sparked a passion for plant-based cooking and nutrition, and I was eager to share my newfound knowledge with others.

As I explored this new lifestyle, I encountered a wealth of information about the environmental and ethical implications of our food choices. It became clear that adopting a plant-based diet was not only beneficial for personal health but also for the planet. The production of plant-based foods generally requires fewer resources and generates lower greenhouse gas emissions compared to animal-based foods. Additionally, a plant-based diet can reduce our reliance on factory farming, which often involves inhumane practices. Understanding these broader impacts reinforced my commitment and made the journey even more meaningful.

Choosing a plant-based lifestyle is more than just a dietary choice; it's a commitment to better health, a cleaner environment, and a more compassionate world. With its easy, tasty, and approachable recipes, this cookbook is perfect for newcomers and will make the switch to a plant-based diet stress-free and pleasurable.

Throughout the book, you'll discover helpful tips on essential ingredients, kitchen tools, and meal prep strategies to make plant-based cooking a breeze. You'll learn how to create balanced meals that meet your nutritional needs and keep you feeling satisfied and energized. Additionally, you'll find practical advice on shopping for plant-based ingredients, understanding nutritional labels, and making the most of seasonal produce.

Embarking on a plant-based lifestyle might feel overwhelming at first, but remember, every small step counts. My goal is to provide you with the knowledge, tools, and confidence to make plant-based eating a joyful and sustainable part of your life. I encourage you to experiment with new ingredients, try out different recipes, and most importantly, enjoy the process.

From hearty breakfasts and vibrant salads to comforting main dishes and delectable desserts, this cookbook covers a wide array of meals to suit any occasion. Whether you're cooking for yourself, your family, or entertaining guests, you'll find recipes that are sure to delight and inspire.

In addition to recipes, this book also includes a section on plant-based nutrition, explaining the benefits of various nutrients and how to ensure you're getting a balanced diet. You'll find information on protein sources, the importance of fiber, essential vitamins and minerals, and tips for maintaining optimal health through plant-based eating.

This cookbook is not just about providing recipes; it's about empowering you to make informed choices and discover a way of eating that is both fulfilling and nourishing. With each recipe, I hope to offer not only a meal but also a moment of joy and a step towards a healthier, more conscious way of living.

I am excited to share these recipes and tips with you, and I hope they inspire you to explore the endless possibilities of plant-based cuisine. Here's to delicious meals, vibrant health, and a better world for all! Let's embark on this journey together and make every meal a celebration of good food and good health. Enjoy the adventure!

Chapter 1: Getting Started with Plant-Based Eating

Understanding Plant-Based Diets

The plant-based diet is gaining momentum as more people recognize the profound health, lifestyle and environment benefits it offers. Rooted in the consumption of whole, unprocessed plant foods, this diet emphasizes fruits, vegetables, legumes, nuts, seeds, and whole grains while minimizing or eliminating animal products and processed foods.

The key philosophy behind a plant-based diet is not about stringent restrictions but about emphasizing nutrient-dense, whole foods that offer a myriad of health benefits. The flexibility of plant-based eating allows individuals to tailor their diet to their personal preferences and nutritional needs, making it a sustainable and enjoyable lifestyle choice.

Benefits of a Plant-Based Diet

Health Benefits:

Weight Management: A diet rich in fruits, vegetables, whole grains, and legumes is typically lower in calories and higher in fiber, promoting feelings of fullness and aiding in weight control. Research indicates that individuals on a plant-based diet often have lower body mass indexes (BMIs) and reduced risks of obesity. These diets can help with weight loss and maintaining a healthy weight due to their high fiber content, which slows digestion and increases satiety.

Longevity: Studies suggest that a diet centered around plant foods can contribute to a longer lifespan. The high antioxidant content in plant foods helps combat oxidative stress, which is linked to aging and chronic diseases. Antioxidants, such as vitamins C and E, flavonoids, and carotenoids, found abundantly in plants, protect cells from damage and support overall health.

Cardiovascular Health: A plant-based diet is known to improve heart health by lowering blood pressure, reducing cholesterol levels, and decreasing the risk of heart disease. The abundance of fiber, healthy fats, and phytonutrients supports cardiovascular function. Plant-based diets are associated with lower cholesterol levels, reduced inflammation, and improved arterial function, all contributing to a healthier heart.

Diabetes Management: Plant-based eating can improve insulin sensitivity and lower the risk of type 2 diabetes. The diet's high fiber content helps regulate blood sugar levels, making it a beneficial choice for diabetes prevention and management. High fiber intake from plant foods also supports a healthy digestive system, preventing rapid spikes in blood sugar and promoting steady energy levels.

Reduced Risk of Chronic Diseases: Plant-based diets are linked to a lower incidence of type 2 diabetes, hypertension, and certain cancers. The combination of high fiber, vitamins, minerals, and antioxidants in plant foods contributes to a reduced risk of chronic diseases by supporting the immune system and reducing inflammation.

Environmental Impact

Reduced Carbon Footprint: Plant-based diets generally require fewer resources and produce fewer greenhouse gases than diets heavy in animal products. By reducing the demand for animal agriculture, plant-based eating contributes to decreased deforestation and habitat destruction, leading to a more sustainable planet. Animal farming is a significant source of methane and other greenhouse gases, so reducing meat consumption can lower overall emissions.

Conservation of Water: Plant-based foods typically use less water to produce compared to meat and dairy. For instance, producing one pound of beef requires approximately 1,800 gallons of water, while growing one pound of vegetables requires around 39 gallons. By choosing plant-based options, individuals can significantly reduce their water footprint.

Ethical Considerations

Animal Welfare: A plant-based diet minimizes harm to animals and reduces reliance on factory farming. Many people choose plant-based eating to avoid contributing to the cruelty and inhumane conditions often found in animal farming practices. This dietary choice supports more humane treatment of animals.

Sustainable Living: Choosing plant-based can contribute to a more sustainable and ethical lifestyle. Beyond health benefits, plant-based eating aligns with values of environmental stewardship and compassion towards animals. It encourages sustainable agricultural practices and reduces the negative impacts of food production on the planet.

Chapter 2: Basics of Plant-Based Nutrition

Understanding Macronutrients and Micronutrients

Transitioning to a plant-based diet is an excellent step toward improved health and well-being. To ensure a balanced and nutritious diet, it's essential to understand the role of macronutrients and micronutrients in your daily meals.

Macronutrients

Macronutrients are the nutrients your body needs in large amounts to function correctly. They include carbohydrates, proteins, and fats.

1. **Carbohydrates**: Carbohydrates are the primary energy source for your body. They fuel your brain, muscles, and other vital organs. There are two types of carbohydrates: simple and complex.

   o **Simple Carbohydrates**: These are quickly digested and found in foods such as fruits and honey. They provide immediate energy but should be consumed in moderation.

   o **Complex Carbohydrates**: Found in whole grains, legumes, and vegetables, these carbs take longer to digest and provide sustained energy. They are also rich in fiber, which aids digestion and helps maintain stable blood sugar levels.

Plant-Based Sources:

Whole Grains: Brown rice, quinoa, oats, barley, millet, buckwheat.
Legumes: Beans (black beans, kidney beans, pinto beans), lentils (green, brown, red), chickpeas, peas.
Vegetables: Sweet potatoes, potatoes, corn, squash, carrots, beets.
Fruits: Apples, bananas, berries (strawberries, blueberries, raspberries), oranges, mangoes, grapes.

2. **Proteins**: Proteins are essential for building and repairing tissues, producing enzymes and hormones, and supporting overall body function. Amino acids, the building blocks of proteins, are either essential (must be obtained from diet) or non-essential (produced by the body).

Complete Proteins: These contain all nine essential amino acids. While many plant foods lack one or more essential amino acids, combining different sources can provide a complete profile.

Plant-Based Sources:

Legumes: Chickpeas, lentils, black beans, kidney beans, pinto beans, soybeans.
Nuts and Seeds: Chia seeds, hemp seeds, flaxseeds, sunflower seeds, pumpkin seeds, almonds, walnuts, cashews, peanuts.
Whole Grains: Quinoa, buckwheat, farro, amaranth.
Soy Products: Tofu, tempeh, edamame, soy milk.
Vegetables: Spinach, kale, broccoli, Brussels sprouts, asparagus.

3. **Fats**: Fats are vital for energy storage, hormone production, and nutrient absorption. There are three main types of fats: saturated, unsaturated, and trans fats.

      ○ **Saturated Fats**: Found in animal products and some plant oils, these should be limited.

      ○ **Unsaturated Fats**: These healthy fats are crucial for heart health and are found in many plant-based foods.

      ○ **Trans Fats**: These are unhealthy fats found in processed foods and should be avoided.

Plant-Based Sources:

Avocados
Nuts: Almonds, walnuts, cashews, pistachios, pecans, macadamia nuts.
Seeds: Flaxseeds, chia seeds, hemp seeds, sunflower seeds, pumpkin seeds.
Oils: Olive oil, coconut oil, avocado oil, flaxseed oil, walnut oil.
Nut Butters: Almond butter, peanut butter, cashew butter.

Micronutrients

Micronutrients are vitamins and minerals required in smaller quantities but are equally important for maintaining health.

4. **Vitamins**:

      ○ **Vitamin B12**: Essential for nerve function and blood formation. Plant-based sources are limited, so fortified foods or supplements are often necessary.

      ○ **Vitamin D**: Important for bone health and immune function. Sun exposure and fortified foods or supplements can help maintain adequate levels.

      ○ **Vitamin C**: A powerful antioxidant that aids in immune function and skin health. Found abundantly in fruits, berries and vegetables.

      ○ **Vitamin A**: Supports vision, immune function, and skin health. Found in carrots, sweet potatoes, and leafy greens.

      ○ **Vitamin K**: Important for blood clotting and bone health. Found in leafy greens like kale and spinach.

Plant-Based Sources:

Vitamin B12: Fortified plant milks, fortified cereals, nutritional yeast.
Vitamin D: Fortified plant milks, mushrooms exposed to sunlight.
Vitamin C: Citrus fruits, strawberries, bell peppers, broccoli, Brussels sprouts, tomatoes.
Vitamin A: Carrots, sweet potatoes, butternut squash, cantaloupe, spinach, kale.
Vitamin K: Kale, spinach, broccoli, Brussels sprouts, green beans.

5. **Minerals**:

- **Iron**: Crucial for blood health and energy production. Plant-based iron (non-heme) is less easily absorbed, so combining with vitamin C-rich foods can enhance absorption.

- **Calcium**: Vital for bone health. Found in fortified plant milks, tofu, almonds, and leafy greens.

- **Zinc**: Important for immune function and wound healing. Found in legumes, nuts, seeds, and whole grains.

- **Magnesium**: Involved in muscle and nerve function, blood sugar control, and bone health. Found in nuts, seeds, whole grains, and leafy greens.

- **Omega-3 Fatty Acids**: Essential for brain health and anti-inflammatory functions. Found in flaxseeds, chia seeds, and walnuts.

Plant-Based Sources:

Iron: Lentils, chickpeas, beans, quinoa, pumpkin seeds, sesame seeds, dark leafy greens (spinach, Swiss chard).
Calcium: Fortified plant milks (almond, soy, oat), tofu, tempeh, almonds, sesame seeds, tahini, bok choy, broccoli.
Zinc: Lentils, chickpeas, black beans, pumpkin seeds, sunflower seeds, cashews, quinoa, oats.
Magnesium: Almonds, cashews, pumpkin seeds, sunflower seeds, chia seeds, flaxseeds, whole grains (brown rice, quinoa), dark leafy greens (spinach, Swiss chard).
Omega-3 Fatty Acids: Flaxseeds, chia seeds, hemp seeds, walnuts, algae oil.

Chapter 3: Essential Ingredients

Transitioning to a plant-based diet is a delightful journey filled with vibrant flavors, nutritious meals, and new culinary adventures. One of the first steps in embracing this lifestyle is stocking your kitchen with essential ingredients.

Grains and Pasta: Quinoa, Amaranth, brown rice, whole wheat pasta, couscous, barley, bulgur, millet, oats, farro, rice noodles

Legumes: Chickpeas, black beans, lentils (green, red, brown), kidney beans, cannellini beans, navy beans, pinto beans, split peas, mung beans

Nuts and Seeds: Almonds, walnuts, cashews, sunflower seeds, chia seeds, flaxseeds, hemp seeds, pumpkin seeds, sesame seeds, pine nuts, pistachios, Brazil nuts

Flours and Baking Essentials: Whole wheat flour, almond flour, chickpea flour, coconut flour, spelt flour, baking powder, baking soda, active dry yeast, cornstarch

Oils and Fats: Extra virgin olive oil, coconut oil, avocado oil, sesame oil, flaxseed oil, nut butters (peanut, almond, cashew), tahini

Sweeteners: Maple syrup, topinambur syrup, agave nectar, coconut sugar, date syrup, stevia, raw sugar

Herbs and Spices: Turmeric, cumin, coriander, paprika, smoked paprika, cinnamon, nutmeg, cloves, cardamom, bay leaves, oregano, thyme, basil, rosemary, dill, mint, parsley, cilantro, sage, chives, garlic powder, onion powder, chili powder, cayenne pepper, black pepper, sea salt, nutritional yeast

Condiments and Sauces: Soy sauce, tamari, mustard, apple cider vinegar, balsamic vinegar, rice vinegar, red wine vinegar, white wine vinegar, tahini

Canned and Jarred Goods: Tomato paste, diced tomatoes, coconut milk, olives, capers

Dried Fruits and Snacks: Raisins, dried apricots, dates, prunes, figs, cranberries, banana chips, trail mix, popcorn, seaweed snacks

Fresh Produce Guide

Fresh fruits and vegetables are the cornerstone of a plant-based diet. They provide essential vitamins, minerals, and fiber while adding vibrant colors and flavors to your meals. Here's a guide to some of the best fresh produce to include in your plant-based diet:

Leafy Greens: Kale, spinach, Swiss chard, collard greens, arugula, romaine lettuce, mixed salad greens

Vegetables: Tomatoes, cucumbers, bell peppers, zucchini, eggplant, carrots, celery, beets, radishes, broccoli, cauliflower, Brussels sprouts, green beans, asparagus, mushrooms, sweet potatoes, regular potatoes, onions, garlic, shallots, leeks.

Fruits: Apples, bananas, oranges, lemons, limes, berries (strawberries, blueberries, raspberries, blackberries), grapes, pears, peaches, plums, nectarines, pineapples, mangoes, avocados

Herbs: Basil, parsley, cilantro, mint, dill, rosemary, thyme, sage, chives

Others: Ginger, turmeric root, fresh chilies, lemongrass, scallions, bean sprouts, sprouts

Stocking your kitchen with these essential ingredients will set you up for success on your plant-based journey. Remember, the key to a successful plant-based diet is variety, so don't be afraid to experiment with different ingredients and recipes to find what you love best.

Foods to Avoid or Limit on a Plant-Based Diet

While focusing on whole plant foods, it's also essential to avoid or limit certain items:

1. **Processed and Refined Foods:** Foods like white bread, pastries, and sugary snacks lack nutritional value and can lead to weight gain, blood sugar spikes, and nutritional deficiencies.
   Challenges and Solutions: Cravings for these foods can be strong. Replace them with whole food alternatives like fruit, whole grain crackers, or homemade baked goods made with whole grains.

2. **Animal Products:** Meat, dairy, and eggs can be high in saturated fats and cholesterol, which may contribute to heart disease and other health issues.
   Challenges and Solutions: Transitioning away from animal products can be difficult. Try plant-based alternatives like almond milk, soy yogurt, and veggie burgers. Gradually reduce animal products to ease the transition.

3. **Added Sugars and Sweets:** Excessive sugar intake can lead to weight gain, diabetes, and other metabolic disorders.
   Challenges and Solutions: Cravings for sweets can be managed by consuming naturally sweet fruits or using small amounts of natural sweeteners like maple syrup or dates.

4. **Refined Oils:** Oils like corn oil, canola oil, and vegetable oil are highly processed and can be high in omega-6 fatty acids, which may promote inflammation.
   Challenges and Solutions: Use whole food fat sources like avocados and nuts, and cook with minimal amounts of healthy oils like olive oil.

Shopping and Storage Tips for a Plant-Based Kitchen

Shopping for and storing plant-based ingredients effectively is crucial for maintaining the freshness and quality of your food, reducing waste, and making meal preparation more efficient.

Shopping Tips

Plan Ahead: Create a meal plan for the week and make a shopping list based on the recipes you plan to cook. This will help you avoid impulse buys and ensure you have everything you need.

Shop Seasonally: Seasonal produce is often fresher, more flavorful, and less expensive. Visit local farmers' markets or check seasonal produce guides to know what's in season.

Buy in Bulk: For non-perishable items like grains, legumes, nuts, and seeds, buying in bulk can save money and reduce packaging waste. Make sure you have proper storage containers at home.

Read Labels: Look for whole foods and minimal ingredients. Avoid items with added sugars, refined grains, and artificial additives. Focus on fiber, protein, and healthy fats.

Prioritize Fresh Produce: When choosing fresh fruits and vegetables, look for vibrant colors and firm textures. Avoid produce with blemishes, mold, or soft spots.

Explore Plant-Based Alternatives: Familiarize yourself with plant-based alternatives for dairy, meat, and other animal products. These can include almond milk, tofu, tempeh, and vegan cheese.

Storage Tips

Properly Store Produce:

Leafy Greens: Store in the refrigerator in a breathable bag or wrap in a damp paper towel and place in a plastic bag.

Root Vegetables: Keep in a cool, dark place. Potatoes, sweet potatoes, and onions should be stored in a pantry or a dedicated vegetable drawer.

Berries and Fruits: Refrigerate berries and most fruits, except for bananas, avocados, and tomatoes, which can be kept at room temperature until ripe.

Use Airtight Containers: Store grains, legumes, nuts, seeds, and dried fruits in airtight containers to keep them fresh and prevent pests.

Freeze for Longevity:

Vegetables: Blanch and freeze vegetables like broccoli, spinach, and green beans to extend their shelf life.

Fruits: Freeze fruits like berries, bananas, and mangoes for smoothies and baking.

Organize Your Pantry: Keep your pantry neat and organized. Use clear containers and label them to easily identify ingredients. Rotate older items to the front so they are used first.

Store Oils Properly: Keep oils in a cool, dark place to prevent them from going rancid. Olive oil, for instance, should be stored in a dark bottle.

Refrigerate Nuts and Seeds: To prolong their freshness and prevent them from becoming rancid, store nuts and seeds in the refrigerator or freezer.

Plan Leftovers: When cooking larger batches, store leftovers in portion-sized containers. Label them with the date and contents to keep track of freshness.

Use Glass Jars: Store homemade sauces, dressings, and nut butters in glass jars. They are durable, non-reactive, and can be easily labeled and organized.

Invest in Quality Storage Bags: Reusable silicone bags are great for storing snacks, cut vegetables, and even liquids. They are eco-friendly and keep food fresh.

Chapter 4: Kitchen Tools and Equipment for a Plant-Based Kitchen

Embarking on a plant-based culinary journey can be exciting and rewarding, especially when equipped with the right tools and equipment. Having the right gadgets at your disposal can simplify meal preparation, enhance your cooking experience, and ensure that your dishes are both delicious and nutritious.

Must-Have Kitchen Gadgets

- **High-Quality Chef's Knife**: A sharp, versatile knife is essential for chopping, dicing, and slicing.
- **Cutting Board**: Having a few sturdy cutting boards is essential. The best material for a board is wood.
- **Blender**: It can be used to make smoothies, soups, sauces, and even nut butters. Look for a blender with multiple speed settings and a robust motor to handle a variety of textures.
- **Food Processor**: Is another versatile tool that can chop, slice, shred, and puree ingredients. Great for making dips, spreads, and doughs.
- **Measuring Cups and Spoons**: Accurate measurements are crucial for recipe success.
- **Mixing Bowls**: Various sizes for mixing ingredients and preparing recipes. Stainless steel or glass bowls are durable and easy to clean.
- **Wooden Spoons and Spatulas:** Wooden utensils are gentle on cookware and ideal for stirring, mixing, and sautéing.
- **Non-Stick Skillet:** A good-quality skillet is essential for sautéing vegetables, making stir-fries, and cooking plant-based proteins.
- **Baking Sheets and Pans:** Baking is a common method in plant-based cooking. Ensure you have a variety of baking sheets and pans, including cookie sheets, muffin tins, and loaf pans. Opt for non-stick or silicone-coated varieties for easy release and cleanup.

Optional Tools for Convenience

- **Slow Cooker**: Makes cooking grains, beans, and stews more convenient.
- **Immersion Blender:** An immersion blender is a convenient tool for blending soups, sauces, and smoothies directly in the pot or containe.
- **Salad Spinner:** Washing and drying leafy greens can be a tedious task. A salad spinner makes this process quick and easy, ensuring your greens are clean and dry, ready for salads and wraps.
- **Citrus Juicer:** A citrus juicer makes it easy to extract juice from fruits and vegetables.
- **Waffle Iron:** A waffle iron is a handy appliance for making homemade waffles. It allows you to cook waffles to your desired level of crispiness and can also be used for other creative recipes, such as making pancakes or grilling sandwiches.

Chapter 5: Tips for Balanced Plant-Based Nutrition

Include a Variety of Fruits
Enjoy a diverse range of fruits to benefit from different vitamins, minerals, and antioxidants. Pair fruits with protein or healthy fats (e.g., apple slices with almond butter) to slow the absorption of sugars and maintain stable energy levels throughout the day.

Combine Carbohydrates with Protein and Fats
Combining carbohydrates with protein and healthy fats helps regulate blood sugar levels and provides sustained energy. For instance, you can combine quinoa (a complex carbohydrate) with black beans (protein) and avocado (healthy fat) for a balanced meal.

Monitor Portion Sizes
Be mindful of portion sizes, especially with high-sugar fruits, to avoid consuming excessive amounts of simple carbohydrates. Balancing portions ensures you maintain a healthy diet without overindulgence.

Stay Hydrated
Drinking plenty of water is essential for digestion and the efficient metabolism of carbohydrates. Aim for at least eight glasses of water a day, and more if you are physically active.

Embrace a Diverse Diet
Ensure your diet includes a variety of foods to cover all nutritional bases. Mix different vegetables, fruits, grains, legumes, nuts, and seeds. Diversity in your diet helps to ensure you receive a wide range of nutrients essential for overall health.

Incorporate Fortified Foods
Include fortified plant-based milks, cereals, and nutritional yeast in your diet to help meet your needs for vitamin B12, vitamin D, and calcium. These nutrients are essential for bone health, energy production, and overall well-being.

Smart Food Pairings
Combine foods to enhance nutrient absorption. For example, pair iron-rich foods like spinach with vitamin C sources like bell peppers or citrus fruits to improve iron absorption.

Consider Supplements
Consider supplements for nutrients that are harder to obtain from plant-based sources alone, such as vitamin B12, vitamin D, and omega-3 fatty acids. Consult with a healthcare professional to determine which supplements may be necessary for you.

Dairy Alternatives
Replace cow's milk with plant-based alternatives such as almond, soy, or oat milk. These options are often fortified with essential nutrients and provide a similar creamy texture.

Legume Substitutions
Use legumes like black beans or chickpeas instead of meat in tacos, stews, and other dishes. Legumes are rich in protein and fiber, making them excellent meat substitutes.

Soaking Legumes
Soaking legumes before cooking can significantly improve their digestibility and reduce cooking time. By soaking beans, lentils, and other legumes in water for several hours or overnight, you help break down complex sugars that can cause digestive discomfort. Always discard the soaking water and rinse the legumes before cooking to ensure the best results.

Whole Grain Choices
Choose for whole grain versions of bread, pasta, and rice. Whole grains provide more fiber and nutrients compared to their refined counterparts, supporting better digestive health and sustained energy levels.

Plant-Based Spreads
Choose plant-based spreads like hummus or avocado instead of butter. These alternatives are rich in healthy fats and add delicious flavors to your meals.

Regular Check-ups
Monitor your nutritional status with regular blood tests to ensure you're meeting your body's needs. Regular check-ups with a healthcare provider can help identify any deficiencies early and allow for timely intervention.

The Benefits of Soaking Seeds and Nuts

Nuts are known to be one of the hardest raw foods to digest. When dry, they are hard and slightly bitter, and even a small amount can make your stomach feel heavy.

Why Does This Happen?

The seeds and nuts you buy are usually in a dormant state. In this form, your body can't absorb them well, and they pass through your system unchanged.

Dry nuts and seeds contain substances called enzyme inhibitors. These inhibitors stop enzymes from working and keep the seed from sprouting too early. They also cause the bitter taste.

When a seed falls from a tree and dries out, it goes to sleep until it gets wet again, like when snow melts in the spring. Nature makes sure seeds don't sprout too early so they can grow properly when conditions are right.

When you soak nuts and seeds, their chemical makeup changes, and they start to sprout.

During this process, complex substances turn into simpler ones. Enzymes start to work, breaking down starch into simple sugars, which makes the sprouts taste slightly sweet. Later, enzymes turn proteins into amino acids, and fats into fatty acids.

These changes make soaked nuts and seeds easier to digest. They become sweeter as the water washes away the inhibitors and the bitterness. You get nutrients in their most accessible form: active enzymes, minerals, flavonoids, vitamins, and antioxidants.

How to Soak Nuts and Seeds?

It's easy: pour drinking water over raw (not roasted) nuts or seeds and leave them for several hours or overnight, depending on the type, at room temperature. In the morning, rinse and drain the water. You don't need to wait for sprouts because soaking alone starts the process. If a sprout appears, the nutritional value starts to decrease because the nutrients are used for growth.

Soaked nuts and seeds can be stored in the refrigerator for about three days. If you rinse, dry them well, and store them in a container with a tight lid, they can last up to a week.

Benefits of Soaked Nuts and Seeds

Soaking nuts and seeds brings them to life. In this state, they taste better and are more nutritious than when dry.

Adding soaked nuts and seeds to your diet can help with digestion and nutrient absorption, making them a great addition to any plant-based diet. Enjoy the improved flavors and health benefits with this simple method.

Embracing the Plant-Based Lifestyle

Adopting a Plant-Based Diet is not only about what you eat but also about how you live.

Regular Physical Activity
Engage in regular exercise, whether it's walking, yoga, or more intense workouts. Physical activity complements a Plant-Based Diet by boosting energy levels and improving overall health.

Sharing Meals
Eating with family and friends can enhance your dining experience. Sharing plant-based meals encourages social bonds and fosters a supportive community around healthy eating.

Planning and Preparing Meals
Invest time in planning and preparing your meals. This can help ensure you have balanced, nutrient-rich options available and can prevent the temptation to opt for less healthy choices.

Mindful Eating
Practice mindful eating by paying attention to your hunger cues and savoring each bite. This can enhance your relationship with food and promote better digestion and satisfaction.

Educating Yourself
Stay informed about plant-based nutrition to ensure you meet your dietary needs. Understanding the nutritional profiles of different foods can help you create well-balanced meals.

Sustainable Choices
Embrace sustainable practices, such as choosing locally-sourced and organic produce when possible. This not only benefits your health but also supports the environment.

Community Involvement
Join plant-based communities or groups. Participating in local events, potlucks, or online forums can provide support and inspiration on your plant-based journey.

Chapter 6: Breakfasts
Smoothies and Smoothie Bowls

Berry Bliss Smoothie Bowl

Prep. time: 10 min   Cook time: 0 min   Serves: 2

INGREDIENTS

- 2 cups frozen mixed berries
- 1 banana, sliced and frozen
- 1/2 cup unsweetened almond milk
- 1 tbsp chia seeds
- 1 tbsp maple syrup (optional)
- 1/2 cup granola (for topping)
- 1/4 cup fresh berries (for topping)
- 2 tbsp shredded coconut (for topping)
- 2 tbsp sliced almonds (for topping)
- 1 tbsp hemp seeds (for topping)

DIRECTIONS

Soak chia seeds: In a small bowl, mix chia seeds with 3 tbsp water and let sit for 5 minutes until gel-like.
Blend smoothie: In a blender, combine frozen mixed berries, frozen banana, almond milk, soaked chia seeds, and maple syrup (if using). Blend until smooth and thick.
Assemble bowls: Divide the smoothie mixture between two bowls.
Add toppings: Top each bowl with granola, fresh berries, shredded coconut, sliced almonds, and hemp seeds.
Serve immediately: Enjoy your nutritious and delicious Berry Bliss Smoothie Bowl.

Topping variations: Add sliced kiwi or a drizzle of nut butter for extra flavor and nutrition.

Per serving: 280 calories, 5g protein, 11g fats, 38g carbs

Green Goddess Smoothie

Prep. time: 5 min   Cook time: 0 min   Serves: 2

INGREDIENTS

- 2 cups fresh spinach
- 1 banana, sliced and frozen
- 1/2 avocado
- 1 cup unsweetened almond milk
- 1 tbsp chia seeds
- 1 tbsp flax seeds
- 1 tbsp maple syrup (optional)
- 1 kiwi, peeled and sliced (for topping, optional)

DIRECTIONS

Soak chia seeds: In a small bowl, mix chia seeds with 3 tbsp water and let sit for 5 minutes until gel-like.
Blend smoothie: In a blender, combine fresh spinach, frozen banana, avocado, almond milk, soaked chia seeds, flax seeds, and maple syrup (if using). Blend until smooth and creamy.
Serve immediately: Pour the smoothie into two glasses.
Optional toppings: Garnish with kiwi slices for an added boost of flavor and nutrition.

Topping variations: Add sliced strawberries or a few fresh mint leaves for extra flavor and nutrition.

Per serving: 220 calories, 5g protein, 12g fats, 25g carbs

Tropical Sunrise Smoothie Bowl

Prep. time: 10 min   Cook time: 0 min   Serves: 2

INGREDIENTS

- 1 cup frozen mango chunks
- 1 cup frozen pineapple chunks
- 1 banana, sliced and frozen
- 1/2 cup unsweetened coconut milk
- 1/2 cup orange juice
- 1 tbsp chia seeds
- 1 tbsp flax seeds
- 1/2 cup granola (for topping)
- 1/4 cup fresh berries (for topping)
- 2 tbsp shredded coconut (for topping)

DIRECTIONS

Soak chia seeds: In a small bowl, mix chia seeds with 3 tbsp water and let sit for 5 minutes until gel-like.
Blend smoothie: In a blender, combine frozen mango, frozen pineapple, frozen banana, coconut milk, orange juice, soaked chia seeds, and flax seeds. Blend until smooth and thick.
Assemble bowls: Divide the smoothie mixture between two bowls.
Add toppings: Top each bowl with granola, fresh berries, and shredded coconut.
Serve immediately: Enjoy your refreshing and nutritious Tropical Sunrise Smoothie Bowl.

Topping variations: Add sliced banana, chopped nuts, or a drizzle of honey for extra flavor and nutrition.

Per serving: 350 calories, 6g protein, 14g fats, 50g carbs

Beetroot Detox Smoothie

Prep. time: 5 min   Cook time: 0 min   Serves: 2

INGREDIENTS

- 1 cup cooked beetroot, chopped
- 1 apple, cored and sliced
- 1 banana, sliced and frozen
- 1 cup unsweetened almond milk
- 1/2 cup water
- 1 tbsp chia seeds
- 1 tbsp lemon juice
- 1 tbsp fresh ginger, grated
- 1 tbsp hemp seeds (for topping)
- 1 tbsp fresh mint leaves (for topping, optional)

DIRECTIONS

Soak chia seeds: In a small bowl, mix chia seeds with 3 tbsp water and let sit for 5 minutes until gel-like.
Blend smoothie: In a blender, combine chopped beetroot, apple, frozen banana, almond milk, water, soaked chia seeds, lemon juice, and grated ginger. Blend until smooth and creamy.
Serve immediately: Pour the smoothie into two glasses.
Optional toppings: Garnish with hemp seeds and fresh mint leaves for an added boost of flavor and nutrition.

Topping variations: Add fresh berries, or a drizzle of maple syrup for extra flavor and nutrition.

Per serving: 180 calories, 4g protein, 4g fats, 38g carbs

Chocolate Almond Butter Smoothie Bowl

Prep. time: 10 min   Cook time: 0 min   Serves: 2

INGREDIENTS

- bananas, sliced and frozen
- 1/2 avocado
- 1 cup unsweetened almond milk
- 2 tbsp almond butter
- 2 tbsp unsweetened cocoa powder
- 1 tbsp chia seeds
- 1 tbsp maple syrup (optional)
- 1/4 cup granola (for topping)
- 2 tbsp sliced almonds (for topping)
- 1/4 cup fresh berries (for topping)

DIRECTIONS

Soak chia seeds: In a small bowl, mix chia seeds with 3 tbsp water and let sit for 5 minutes until gel-like.

Blend smoothie: In a blender, combine frozen bananas, avocado, almond milk, almond butter, cocoa powder, soaked chia seeds, and maple syrup (if using). Blend until smooth and creamy.

Assemble bowls: Divide the smoothie mixture between two bowls.

Add toppings: Top each bowl with granola, sliced almonds, and fresh berries.

Serve immediately: Enjoy your nutritious and delicious Chocolate Almond Butter Smoothie Bowl.

Topping variations: Add shredded coconut, hemp seeds, or a drizzle of extra almond butter for extra flavor and nutrition.

Per serving: 350 calories, 8g protein, 18g fats, 42g carbs

Banana Oatmeal Breakfast Smoothie

Prep. time: 10 min   Cook time: 0 min   Serves: 2

INGREDIENTS

- 2 bananas, sliced and frozen
- 1/2 cup rolled oats
- 1 cup unsweetened almond milk
- 1 tbsp chia seeds
- 1 tbsp almond butter
- 1/2 tsp cinnamon
- 1 tbsp maple syrup (optional)
- 1/4 cup fresh berries (for topping, optional)
- 1 tbsp hemp seeds (for topping, optional)
- 1 tbsp sliced almonds (for topping, optional)

DIRECTIONS

Soak chia seeds: In a small bowl, mix chia seeds with 3 tbsp water and let sit for 5 minutes until gel-like.

Blend smoothie: In a blender, combine frozen bananas, rolled oats, almond milk, soaked chia seeds, almond butter, cinnamon, and maple syrup (if using). Blend until smooth and creamy.

Assemble bowls: Divide the smoothie mixture between two bowls.

Add toppings: Top each bowl with fresh berries, sliced almonds, and hemp seeds.

Serve immediately: Enjoy your nutritious and delicious Banana Oatmeal Breakfast Smoothie Bowl.

Topping variations: Add sliced banana, a sprinkle of cacao nibs, or a drizzle of additional almond butter for extra flavor and nutrition.

Per serving: 330 calories, 7g protein, 12g fats, 45g carbs

Banana Cinnamon Apple Pie Overnight Oats

Prep. time: 10 min   Cook time: 0 min   Serves: 2

INGREDIENTS

- 1 cup rolled oats
- 1 cup unsweetened almond milk
- 1 apple, diced
- 1 banana, mashed
- 1 tbsp chia seeds
- 1 tsp cinnamon
- 1/2 tsp vanilla extract
- 1 tbsp maple syrup (optional)
- 2 tbsp chopped walnuts (for topping, optional)
- 1/4 cup fresh apple slices (for topping, optional)

DIRECTIONS

Instructions: Combine ingredients: In a bowl, mix rolled oats, almond milk, diced apple, mashed banana, chia seeds, cinnamon, vanilla extract, and maple syrup (if using).
Refrigerate: Cover the bowl and refrigerate overnight, or for at least 4 hours.
Serve: Stir the oats and divide between two bowls or jars.
Optional toppings: Garnish with chopped walnuts and fresh apple slices for added flavor and nutrition.
Serve immediately: Enjoy your nutritious and delicious Banana Cinnamon Apple Pie Overnight Oats.

Topping variations: Add a drizzle of almond butter, a sprinkle of ground flaxseed, or a handful of raisins for extra flavor and nutrition.

Per serving: 320 calories, 6g protein, 10g fats, 52g carbs

Berry Burst Overnight Oats

Prep. time: 5 min   Cook time: 0 min   Serves: 2

INGREDIENTS

- 1 cup rolled oats
- 1 cup unsweetened almond milk
- 1/2 cup mixed berries (fresh or frozen)
- 1 banana, mashed
- 1 tbsp chia seeds
- 1 tbsp maple syrup
- 1/2 tsp vanilla extract
- 1/4 cup chopped walnuts (for topping)
- 2 tbsp hemp seeds (for topping, optional)
- 1/4 cup additional fresh berries (for topping, optional)

DIRECTIONS

Combine ingredients: In a bowl, mix rolled oats, almond milk, mixed berries, mashed banana, chia seeds, maple syrup, and vanilla extract.
Refrigerate: Cover the bowl and refrigerate overnight, or for at least 4 hours.
Serve: Stir the oats and divide between two bowls or jars.
Optional toppings: Garnish with chopped walnuts, hemp seeds, and additional fresh berries for added flavor and nutrition.
Serve immediately: Enjoy your nutritious and delicious Berry Burst Overnight Oats.

Topping variations: Add a drizzle of almond butter, a sprinkle of flax seeds, or a handful of granola for extra flavor and nutrition.

Per serving: 310 calories, 8g protein, 12g fats, 44g carbs

Peanut Butter Banana Chia Pudding

INGREDIENTS

Prep. time: 5 min   Cook time: 0 min   Serves: 2

- 1/4 cup chia seeds
- 1 1/2 cups unsweetened almond milk
- 2 tbsp peanut butter
- 1 banana, mashed
- 1 tbsp maple syrup
- 1/2 tsp vanilla extract
- 1/4 cup sliced banana (for topping)
- 2 tbsp chopped peanuts (for topping)
- 1 tbsp cocoa nibs (for topping, optional)
- 1/4 cup fresh berries (for topping, optional)

DIRECTIONS

Combine ingredients: In a bowl, mix chia seeds, almond milk, peanut butter, mashed banana, maple syrup, and vanilla extract until well combined.
Refrigerate: Cover and refrigerate overnight, or for at least 4 hours, until the mixture thickens into a pudding-like consistency.
Serve: Stir the chia pudding and divide between two bowls or jars.
Optional toppings: Garnish with sliced banana, chopped peanuts, cocoa nibs, and fresh berries for added flavor and nutrition.
Serve immediately: Enjoy your nutritious and delicious Peanut Butter Banana Chia Pudding.

Topping variations: Add a drizzle of additional peanut butter, a sprinkle of granola, or a few slices of kiwi for extra flavor and nutrition.

Per serving: 320 calories, 10g protein, 18g fats, 28g carbs

Blueberry Lemon Chia Pudding

INGREDIENTS

Prep. time: 5 min   Cook time: 0 min   Serves: 2

- 1/4 cup chia seeds
- 1 1/2 cups unsweetened almond milk
- 1/2 cup fresh or frozen blueberries
- 2 tbsp maple syrup
- 1 tsp lemon zest
- 1 tbsp lemon juice
- 1/2 tsp vanilla extract
- 1/4 cup fresh blueberries (for topping)
- 2 tbsp sliced almonds (for topping)
- 1 tbsp shredded coconut (for topping, optional)

DIRECTIONS

Combine ingredients: In a bowl, mix chia seeds, almond milk, blueberries, maple syrup, lemon zest, lemon juice, and vanilla extract until well combined.
Refrigerate: Cover and refrigerate overnight, or for at least 4 hours, until the mixture thickens into a pudding-like consistency.
Serve: Stir the chia pudding and divide between two bowls or jars.
Optional toppings: Garnish with fresh blueberries, sliced almonds, and shredded coconut for added flavor and nutrition.
Serve immediately: Enjoy your nutritious and delicious Blueberry Lemon Chia Pudding.

Topping variations: Add a drizzle of almond butter, a sprinkle of granola, or a few mint leaves for extra flavor and nutrition.

Per serving: 250 calories, 6g protein, 12g fats, 30g carbs

Flaxseed Porridge with Banana

INGREDIENTS

Prep. time: 10 min   Cook time: 0 min   Serves: 2

- 6 tbsp flax seeds
- 2 bananas
- 100 ml oat milk
- 2 tsp peanut butter
- 2 tsp coconut flakes
- 20 g pumpkin seeds
- 1 tsp maple syrup

DIRECTIONS

Soak flax seeds: Rinse the flax seeds and soak them in a glass with 250 ml of water overnight.
Blend ingredients: Place the flax seeds in a blender with the soaking water. Add oat milk, maples syrup, peanut butter, and coconut flakes. Blend well until smooth. Pour the mixture into two bowls.
Add banana: Cut the bananas into cubes and mix them into the porridge. Enjoy your delicious and nutritious flaxseed porridge.

Topping variations: Add fresh berries, a sprinkle of chia seeds, or a drizzle of maple syrup for extra flavor and nutrition.

Per serving: 350 calories, 17g protein, 30g fats, 46g carbs

Sesame Porridge with Lemon

INGREDIENTS

Prep. time: 5 min   Cook time: 0 min   Serves: 2

- 8 tbsp sesame seeds
- 2 bananas
- 1 apple or pear
- Juice of or 1/2 lemon
- 2 thin slices of lime or lemon with zest
- 2 tsp tahini (optional)
- 200 ml water (for blending)
- Sesame seeds (for topping)
- Lemon zest (for topping)
- Almonds (for topping)

DIRECTIONS

Soak sesame seeds: Soak the sesame seeds in a glass with 200 ml of water overnight.
Blend ingredients: In a blender, combine soaked sesame seeds, one banana, apple or pear, lime or lemon juice, lime or lemon slices, tahini (if using), and water. Blend until smooth.
Serve: Pour the mixture into two bowls.
Optional toppings: Garnish with the remaining banana slices, sesame seeds, lemon zest, and almonds for added flavor and nutrition.
Serve immediately: Enjoy your nutritious and delicious Sesame Porridge with Lemon.

Topping variations: Add fresh berries, a drizzle of maple syrup, or a sprinkle of chia seeds for extra flavor and nutrition.

Per serving: 320 calories, 8g protein, 15g fats, 35g carbs

Classic Avocado Toast

Prep. time: 10 min   Cook time: 0 min   Serves: 2

INGREDIENTS

- 2 slices whole grain bread
- 1 ripe avocado
- 1/2 lemon, juiced
- 1 small tomato, diced
- 2 tbsp hemp seeds
- 1 tbsp olive oil
- Salt and pepper to taste
- Fresh basil leaves (for topping, optional)
- Red pepper flakes (for topping, optional)

DIRECTIONS

Prepare avocado: Mash the avocado in a bowl with lemon juice, salt, and pepper.
Toast bread: Toast the whole grain bread slices until golden brown.
Assemble toast: Spread the mashed avocado evenly on each slice of toasted bread.
Add toppings: Top with diced tomato, hemp seeds, and drizzle with olive oil.
Optional garnishes: Add fresh basil leaves and a sprinkle of red pepper flakes for extra flavor and nutrition.
Serve immediately: Enjoy your nutritious and delicious Classic Avocado Toast.

Topping variations: Add sliced radishes, a sprinkle of nutritional yeast, or a few slices of cucumber for extra flavor and nutrition.

Per serving: 300 calories, 6g protein, 22g fats, 28g carbs

Mushroom and Spinach Tofu Scramble

Prep. time: 10 min   Cook time: 10 min   Serves: 2

INGREDIENTS

- 1 block (200g) firm tofu, drained and crumbled
- 1 cup mushrooms, sliced
- 2 cups fresh spinach
- 1 small onion, diced
- 1 clove garlic, minced
- 1 tbsp olive oil
- 1/2 tsp turmeric
- 1/2 tsp paprika
- Salt and pepper to taste
- 1 tbsp nutritional yeast (optional)

DIRECTIONS

Cook vegetables: In a large pan, heat olive oil over medium heat. Add onions and garlic, and cook until translucent.
Add mushrooms: Add sliced mushrooms to the pan and cook until they release their moisture and start to brown.
Add tofu: Add the crumbled tofu to the pan, along with turmeric, paprika, salt, and pepper. Stir well to combine and heat through.
Add spinach: Add fresh spinach and cook until wilted.
Optional: Stir in nutritional yeast for a cheesy flavor.
Serve immediately: Divide the scramble between two plates and enjoy your nutritious and delicious Mushroom and Spinach Tofu Scramble.

Topping variations: Garnish with fresh herbs, avocado slices, or a squeeze of lemon juice for extra flavor and nutrition.

Per serving: 250 calories, 14g protein, 16g fats, 12g carbs

Burrito with Black Beans

Prep. time: 10 min   Cook time: 10 min   Serves: 2

INGREDIENTS

- 1 cup black beans, cooked and drained
- 1 cup diced tomatoes
- 1 cup spinach, chopped
- 1 small onion, diced
- 1 clove garlic, minced
- 1 avocado, sliced
- 2 whole grain tortillas
- 1 tbsp olive oil
- 1 tsp cumin
- Salt and pepper to taste

DIRECTIONS

Cook vegetables: Heat olive oil in a pan over medium heat. Add onion and garlic, and cook until translucent.
Add beans and tomatoes: Add black beans, diced tomatoes, cumin, salt, and pepper. Cook for 5 minutes until heated through.
Add spinach: Stir in chopped spinach and cook until wilted.
Assemble burritos: Warm tortillas in a pan or microwave. Divide the bean mixture between the two tortillas, and top with avocado slices.
Wrap and serve: Roll up the tortillas to form burritos and serve immediately.
Optional toppings: Add a squeeze of lime juice, fresh cilantro, or a drizzle of hot sauce for extra flavor and nutrition.

Per serving: 350 calories, 10g protein, 18g fats, 40g carbs

Chickpea & Avocado Breakfast Toast

Prep. time: 10 min   Cook time: 0 min   Serves: 2

INGREDIENTS

- 1 avocado, mashed
- 1 cup chickpeas, rinsed and mashed
- 1 tbsp lemon juice
- 1 small garlic clove, minced
- 2 slices whole grain bread, toasted
- 1/4 tsp cumin
- 1/4 tsp paprika
- Salt and pepper to taste
- 2 tbsp chopped fresh parsley (optional)
- Red pepper flakes (optional)

DIRECTIONS

Mash chickpeas and avocado: In a bowl, combine mashed avocado, mashed chickpeas, lemon juice, minced garlic, cumin, paprika, salt, and pepper. Mix until well combined.
Prepare toast: Toast the whole grain bread slices until golden brown.
Assemble toast: Spread the chickpea and avocado mixture evenly on each slice of toasted bread.
Optional toppings: Garnish with chopped fresh parsley and a sprinkle of red pepper flakes for added flavor and nutrition.
Serve immediately: Enjoy your nutritious and delicious Chickpea & Avocado Breakfast Toast.

Topping variations: Add sliced tomatoes, radishes, or a drizzle of olive oil for extra flavor and nutrition.

Per serving: 350 calories, 10g protein, 18g fats, 38g carbs

Warm Cinnamon Quinoa Porridge

INGREDIENTS

Prep. time: 5 min   Cook time: 15 min   Serves: 2

- 1 cup quinoa, rinsed
- 2 cups unsweetened almond milk
- 1 tbsp maple syrup
- 1 tsp ground cinnamon
- 1/2 tsp vanilla extract
- 1/4 tsp ground nutmeg
- 1 banana, sliced (for topping)
- 1/4 cup fresh berries (for topping)
- 2 tbsp chopped nuts (for topping)
- 1 tbsp chia seeds (for topping)

DIRECTIONS

Cook quinoa: In a saucepan, combine rinsed quinoa and almond milk. Bring to a boil, then reduce heat and simmer for 15 minutes, or until quinoa is tender and the liquid is absorbed.
Add flavor: Stir in maple syrup, ground cinnamon, vanilla extract, and ground nutmeg.
Serve: Divide the quinoa porridge between two bowls.
Optional toppings: Top with sliced banana, fresh berries, chopped nuts, and chia seeds for added flavor and nutrition.
Serve immediately: Enjoy your nutritious and delicious Warm Cinnamon Quinoa Porridge.

Topping variations: Add a drizzle of almond butter, a sprinkle of flax seeds, or a few dried fruits for extra flavor and nutrition.

Per serving: 350 calories, 10g protein, 12g fats, 50g carbs

Blueberry Almond Amaranth Porridge

INGREDIENTS

Prep. time: 5 min   Cook time: 20 min   Serves: 2

- 1 cup amaranth
- 2 cups unsweetened almond milk
- 1 tbsp maple syrup
- 1 tsp vanilla extract
- 1/2 tsp ground cinnamon
- 1/2 cup fresh blueberries
- 2 tbsp sliced almonds
- 1 tbsp chia seeds (for topping)
- 1/4 cup fresh blueberries (for topping)
- 2 tbsp almond butter (for topping)

DIRECTIONS

Cook amaranth: In a saucepan, combine amaranth and almond milk. Bring to a boil, then reduce heat and simmer for 20 minutes, or until amaranth is tender and the liquid is absorbed.
Add flavor: Stir in maple syrup, vanilla extract, and ground cinnamon.
Add blueberries: Fold in 1/2 cup fresh blueberries.
Serve: Divide the amaranth porridge between two bowls.
Optional toppings: Top with chia seeds, additional fresh blueberries, sliced almonds, and a drizzle of almond butter for added flavor and nutrition.
Serve immediately: Enjoy your nutritious and delicious Blueberry Almond Amaranth Porridge.

Topping variations: Add a sprinkle of flax seeds, a handful of granola, or a few dried fruits for extra flavor and nutrition.

Per serving: 360 calories, 10g protein, 14g fats, 50g carbs

Fluffy Vegan Blueberry Pancakes

INGREDIENTS

Prep. time: 10 min   Cook time: 10 min   Serves: 2

- 1 cup all-purpose flour
- 1 tbsp baking powder
- 1 tbsp sugar
- 1/2 tsp salt
- 1 cup unsweetened almond milk
- 1 tbsp apple cider vinegar
- 1 tsp vanilla extract
- 1 tbsp coconut oil
- 1/2 cup fresh blueberries
- Maple syrup (for topping, optional)

DIRECTIONS

Mix dry ingredients: In a bowl, combine flour, baking powder, sugar, and salt.
Mix wet ingredients: In another bowl, whisk together almond milk, apple cider vinegar, vanilla extract, and coconut oil.
Combine and fold: Mix wet and dry ingredients until just combined, then fold in blueberries.
Cook pancakes: Pour 1/4 cup batter onto a heated non-stick skillet. Cook until bubbles form, flip, and cook until golden brown.
Serve immediately: Stack pancakes and drizzle with maple syrup.
Optional toppings: Add extra blueberries, sliced bananas, or chopped nuts.

Topping variations: Add sliced bananas, a handful of berries, chopped nuts for extra flavor and nutrition.

Per serving: 300 calories, 6g protein, 8g fats, 48g carbs

Vanilla Chia Seed Pancakes

INGREDIENTS

Prep. time: 10 min   Cook time: 10 min   Serves: 2

- 1 cup all-purpose flour
- 1 tbsp chia seeds
- 1 tbsp baking powder
- 1 tbsp sugar
- 1/2 tsp salt
- 1 cup unsweetened almond milk
- 1 tbsp apple cider vinegar
- 1 tsp vanilla extract
- 1 tbsp coconut oil, melted
- Maple syrup (for topping, optional)

DIRECTIONS

Mix dry ingredients: In a bowl, combine flour, chia seeds, baking powder, sugar, and salt.
Mix wet ingredients: In another bowl, whisk together almond milk, apple cider vinegar, vanilla extract, and melted coconut oil.
Combine and mix: Pour the wet ingredients into the dry ingredients and mix until just combined.
Cook pancakes: Pour 1/4 cup batter onto a heated non-stick skillet. Cook until bubbles form, flip, and cook until golden brown.
Serve immediately: Stack pancakes on a plate.
Optional toppings: Drizzle with maple syrup and add fresh fruit, sliced almonds, a dollop of coconut yogurt, or a sprinkle of cinnamon for added flavor and nutrition.

Topping variations: Add sliced bananas, a handful of berries or a drizzle of almond butter for extra flavor and nutrition.

Per serving: 320 calories, 7g protein, 10g fats, 50g carbs

Banana Tofu Pancakes

INGREDIENTS

Prep. time: 10 min   Cook time: 10 min   Serves: 2

- 1 ripe banana
- 1/2 cup silken tofu
- 1 cup all-purpose flour
- 1 tbsp baking powder
- 1 tbsp maple syrup
- 1/2 tsp salt
- 1 cup unsweetened almond milk
- 1 tsp vanilla extract
- 1 tbsp coconut oil, melted

DIRECTIONS

Blend wet ingredients: In a blender, combine banana, silken tofu, almond milk, vanilla extract, and maple syrup until smooth.
Mix dry ingredients: In a bowl, combine flour, baking powder, and salt.
Combine and mix: Pour the wet ingredients into the dry ingredients and mix until just combined. Stir in melted coconut oil.
Cook pancakes: Pour 1/4 cup batter onto a heated non-stick skillet. Cook until bubbles form, flip, and cook until golden brown.
Serve immediately: Stack pancakes on a plate.
Optional toppings: Drizzle with additional maple syrup and add fresh fruit, nuts, or a sprinkle of cinnamon for added flavor and nutrition.

Topping variations: Add a handful of berries or a drizzle of almond butter for extra flavor and nutrition.

Per serving: 340 calories, 9g protein, 12g fats, 50g carbs

Chocolate Chip Oatmeal Pancakes

INGREDIENTS

Prep. time: 10 min   Cook time: 10 min   Serves: 2

- 1 cup rolled oats
- 1 cup unsweetened almond milk
- 1 ripe banana, mashed
- 1 tbsp baking powder
- 1 tbsp maple syrup
- 1 tsp vanilla extract
- 1/2 cup whole wheat flour
- 1/4 cup dairy-free chocolate chips
- 1/4 tsp salt
- 1 tbsp coconut oil (for cooking)

DIRECTIONS

Blend oats: Blend rolled oats in a blender until they form a flour-like consistency.
Mix wet ingredients: In a bowl, combine almond milk, mashed banana, maple syrup, and vanilla extract.
Combine dry ingredients: In another bowl, mix oat flour, whole wheat flour, baking powder, and salt.
Combine mixtures: Pour wet ingredients into dry ingredients and mix until just combined. Fold in chocolate chips.
Cook pancakes: Heat coconut oil in a non-stick skillet over medium heat. Pour 1/4 cup batter onto the skillet, cook until bubbles form, flip, and cook until golden brown.
Serve immediately: Stack pancakes on a plate.
Optional toppings: Drizzle with additional maple syrup and add fresh fruit, nuts, or a sprinkle of cinnamon.

Topping variations: Add sliced bananas, a drizzle of almond butter, or a dollop of coconut yogurt for extra flavor and nutrition.

Per serving: 350 calories, 8g protein, 14g fats, 50g carbs

Savory Chickpea Flour Waffles

Prep. time: 10 min   Cook time: 10 min   Serves: 2

INGREDIENTS

- 1 cup chickpea flour
- 1/2 cup water
- 1/2 cup unsweetened almond milk
- 1 tbsp olive oil
- 1 tsp baking powder
- 1/2 tsp salt
- 1/4 tsp turmeric
- 1/4 tsp black pepper
- 1/4 cup chopped spinach
- 1/4 cup diced red bell pepper

DIRECTIONS

Mix dry ingredients: In a bowl, combine chickpea flour, baking powder, salt, turmeric, and black pepper.
Mix wet ingredients: In another bowl, whisk together water, almond milk, and olive oil.
Combine mixtures: Pour wet ingredients into dry ingredients and mix until smooth. Fold in chopped spinach and red bell pepper.
Preheat waffle iron: Preheat your waffle iron according to the manufacturer's instructions.
Cook waffles: Pour batter into the preheated waffle iron and cook until golden brown and crispy.
Serve immediately: Serve waffles warm.
Optional toppings: Top with avocado slices, cherry tomatoes, fresh herbs, or a drizzle of tahini for added flavor and nutrition.

Topping variations: Add a dollop of hummus, a handful of arugula, or a sprinkle of sesame seeds for extra flavor and nutrition.

Per serving: 250 calories, 10g protein, 10g fats, 30g carbs

Crispy Almond Flour Waffles

Prep. time: 10 min   Cook time: 10 min   Serves: 2

INGREDIENTS

- 1 cup almond flour
- 1/4 cup oat flour
- 1/4 cup unsweetened almond milk
- 1 tbsp ground flaxseed
- 3 tbsp water
- 1 tbsp maple syrup
- 1 tsp baking powder
- 1/2 tsp vanilla extract
- 1/4 tsp salt
- 1 tbsp coconut oil, melted

DIRECTIONS

Prepare flax egg: Mix ground flaxseed with 3 tbsp water and let sit for 5 minutes until gel-like.
Mix dry ingredients: Combine almond flour, oat flour, baking powder, and salt in a large bowl.
Mix wet ingredients: Whisk almond milk, maple syrup, vanilla extract, melted coconut oil, and flax egg in another bowl.
Combine mixtures: Pour wet ingredients into dry ingredients and mix until smooth.
Preheat waffle iron: Preheat waffle iron according to the manufacturer's instructions.
Cook waffles: Pour batter into the waffle iron and cook until golden brown and crispy.
Serve immediately: Serve waffles warm.
Optional toppings: Add fresh berries, sliced bananas, almond butter, chopped nuts, or coconut flakes.

Topping variations: Add coconut yogurt, cinnamon.

Per serving: 320 calories, 9g protein, 24g fats, 16g carbs

Chia and Flaxseed Bread

Prep. time: 15 min   Cook time: 50 min   Serves: 4

INGREDIENTS

- 1 cup whole wheat flour
- 1 cup almond flour
- 1/2 cup chia seeds
- 1/2 cup ground flaxseed
- 2 tsp baking powder
- 1 tsp baking soda
- 1 tsp salt
- 2 cups unsweetened almond milk
- 4 tbsp maple syrup
- 2 tbsp apple cider vinegar

DIRECTIONS

Preheat oven: Preheat your oven to 350°F (175°C) and grease a loaf pan.
Mix dry ingredients: In a large bowl, combine whole wheat flour, almond flour, ground flaxseed, chia seeds, baking powder, baking soda, and salt.
Combine wet ingredients: In another bowl, mix almond milk, maple syrup, and apple cider vinegar.
Mix and fold: Pour wet ingredients into dry ingredients and mix until just combined.
Bake: Pour the batter into the greased loaf pan and bake for 50 minutes, or until a toothpick inserted into the center comes out clean.
Cool and serve: Let the bread cool in the pan for 10 minutes before transferring to a wire rack to cool completely.
Serve: Slice and enjoy your nutritious and delicious Bread.

Per serving: 250 calories, 8g protein, 12g fats, 28g carbs

Classic Vegan Banana Bread

Prep. time: 10 min   Cook time: 50 min   Serves: 4

INGREDIENTS

- 2 ripe bananas, mashed
- 1 cup whole wheat flour
- 1/2 cup almond flour
- 1/4 cup maple syrup
- 1/4 cup unsweetened almond milk
- 2 tbsp coconut oil, melted
- 1 tsp baking powder
- 1/2 tsp baking soda
- 1 tsp vanilla extract
- 1/4 tsp salt

DIRECTIONS

Preheat oven: Preheat your oven to 350°F (175°C) and grease a loaf pan.
Mix wet ingredients: In a bowl, combine mashed bananas, maple syrup, almond milk, melted coconut oil, and vanilla extract.
Mix dry ingredients: In another bowl, combine whole wheat flour, almond flour, baking powder, baking soda, and salt.
Combine and mix: Pour the wet ingredients into the dry ingredients and mix until just combined.
Bake: Pour the batter into the greased loaf pan and bake for 50 minutes, or until a toothpick inserted into the center comes out clean.
Cool and serve: Let the bread cool in the pan for 10 minutes before transferring to a wire rack to cool completely.
Optional toppings: Add nuts, seeds, or chocolate chips to the batter, or sprinkle with oats before baking for added flavor and nutrition.

Per serving: 300 calories, 6g protein, 12g fats, 45g carbs

Tropical Fruit and Nut Granola

Prep. time: 10 min   Cook time: 20 min   Serves: 2

INGREDIENTS

- 1 cup rolled oats
- 1/2 cup chopped dried pineapple
- 1/2 cup chopped dried mango
- 1/4 cup shredded coconut
- 1/2 cup mixed nuts (almonds, cashews, and macadamia nuts), chopped
- 2 tbsp chia seeds
- 1/4 cup maple syrup
- 2 tbsp coconut oil, melted
- 1/2 tsp vanilla extract
- 1/4 tsp salt

DIRECTIONS

Preheat oven: Preheat your oven to 325°F (160°C) and line a baking sheet with parchment paper.
Mix dry ingredients: In a large bowl, combine rolled oats, chopped dried pineapple, chopped dried mango, shredded coconut, mixed nuts, and chia seeds.
Mix wet ingredients: In another bowl, whisk together maple syrup, melted coconut oil, vanilla extract, and salt.
Combine mixtures: Pour the wet ingredients over the dry ingredients and mix until everything is well coated.
Bake: Spread the mixture evenly on the prepared baking sheet and bake for 20 minutes, stirring halfway through, until golden brown.
Cool and serve: Let the granola cool completely before serving.
Optional toppings: Add fresh tropical fruits like banana slices or papaya chunks for extra flavor and nutrition.

Topping variations: Add kiwi slices, a dollop of coconut yogurt.

Per serving: 350 calories, 8g protein, 18g fats, 42g carbs

Crunchy Almond Maple Granola

Prep. time: 10 min   Cook time: 20 min   Serves: 2

INGREDIENTS

- 1 cup rolled oats
- 1/2 cup sliced almonds
- 2 tbsp chia seeds
- 2 tbsp flaxseeds
- 1/4 cup maple syrup
- 2 tbsp coconut oil, melted
- 1/2 tsp vanilla extract
- 1/4 tsp salt
- 1/4 tsp ground cinnamon
- 1/4 cup dried cranberries (optional)

DIRECTIONS

Preheat oven: Preheat your oven to 325°F (160°C) and line a baking sheet with parchment paper.
Mix dry ingredients: In a large bowl, combine rolled oats, sliced almonds, chia seeds, flaxseeds, salt, and ground cinnamon.
Mix wet ingredients: In another bowl, whisk together maple syrup, melted coconut oil, and vanilla extract.
Combine mixtures: Pour the wet ingredients over the dry ingredients and mix until everything is well coated.
Bake: Spread the mixture evenly on the prepared baking sheet and bake for 20 minutes, stirring halfway through, until golden brown and crispy.
Cool and serve: Let the granola cool completely before serving or storing.
Optional toppings: Add dried cranberries or other dried fruits for extra flavor and nutrition.

Topping variations: Sprinkle with fresh berries, a dollop of plant-based yogurt, or a drizzle of almond butter.

Per serving: 300 calories, 8g protein, 16g fats, 34g carbs

Chapter 7: Snacks and Appetizers
Quick and Healthy Snacks

Crispy Baked Chickpea Snacks

Prep. time: 5 min   Cook time: 40 min   Serves: 2

INGREDIENTS

- 1 can (15 oz) chickpeas, rinsed and drained
- 1 tbsp olive oil
- 1/2 tsp garlic powder
- 1/2 tsp paprika
- 1/2 tsp cumin
- 1/2 tsp salt
- 1/4 tsp black pepper

DIRECTIONS

Preheat oven: Preheat your oven to 400°F (200°C) and line a baking sheet with parchment paper.
Dry chickpeas: Pat the chickpeas dry with a paper towel to remove excess moisture.
Season chickpeas: In a bowl, toss the chickpeas with olive oil, garlic powder, paprika, cumin, salt, and black pepper until evenly coated.
Bake: Spread the chickpeas in a single layer on the prepared baking sheet and bake for 40 minutes, stirring halfway through, until crispy and golden brown.
Cool and serve: Let the chickpeas cool slightly before serving.
Optional toppings: Sprinkle with nutritional yeast, lemon zest, or fresh herbs for added flavor and nutrition.

Topping variations: Add a pinch of cayenne pepper for extra spice, or drizzle with tahini for a creamy finish.

Per serving: 180 calories, 8g protein, 7g fats, 22g carbs

Savory Kale Chips

Prep. time: 10 min   Cook time: 20 min   Serves: 2

INGREDIENTS

- 1 bunch kale, washed and dried
- 1 tbsp olive oil
- 2 tbsp nutritional yeast
- 1/2 tsp garlic powder
- 1/2 tsp smoked paprika
- 1/4 tsp salt
- 1/4 tsp black pepper

DIRECTIONS

Preheat oven: Preheat your oven to 300°F (150°C) and line a baking sheet with parchment paper.
Prepare kale: Remove the kale leaves from the stems and tear into bite-sized pieces.
Mix seasoning: In a large bowl, toss the kale with olive oil, nutritional yeast, garlic powder, smoked paprika, salt, and black pepper until evenly coated.
Bake: Spread the kale pieces in a single layer on the baking sheet and bake for 20 minutes, or until crispy, flipping halfway through.
Cool and serve: Let the kale chips cool slightly before serving.
Optional toppings: Sprinkle with sesame seeds, red pepper flakes, lemon zest, or a dash of hot sauce for extra flavor.

Topping variations: Add hemp seeds, a drizzle of tahini.

Per serving: 120 calories, 5g protein, 7g fats, 10g carbs

Coconut Cashew Energy Balls

Prep. time: 10 min	Cook time: 0 min	Serves: 2

INGREDIENTS

- 1 cup cashews
- 1/2 cup shredded coconut
- 1/4 cup rolled oats
- 2 tbsp maple syrup
- 1 tbsp coconut oil
- 1/2 tsp vanilla extract
- 1/4 tsp salt
- 1/4 cup dried cranberries (optional)
- 1/4 cup dark chocolate chips (optional)
- Additional shredded coconut for rolling (optional)

DIRECTIONS

Blend ingredients: In a food processor, combine cashews, shredded coconut, rolled oats, maple syrup, coconut oil, vanilla extract, and salt. Process until the mixture is well combined and sticky.

Add optional ingredients: If using, add dried cranberries and dark chocolate chips to the mixture and pulse a few times to incorporate.

Form balls: Scoop out small portions of the mixture and roll into balls using your hands.

Roll in coconut: Roll each ball in additional shredded coconut if desired.

Chill: Place the energy balls in the refrigerator for at least 30 minutes to firm up.

Serve: Enjoy your nutritious and delicious Energy Balls.

Topping variations: Roll in cocoa powder or crushed nuts.

Per serving: 250 calories, 5g protein, 18g fats, 18g carbs

Pumpkin Spice Energy Balls

Prep. time: 10 min	Cook time: 0 min	Serves: 2

INGREDIENTS

- 1/2 cup rolled oats
- 1/2 cup almond flour
- 1/4 cup pumpkin puree
- 1/4 cup almond butter
- 2 tbsp maple syrup
- 1 tsp pumpkin spice mix
- 1/2 tsp vanilla extract
- 1/4 cup chopped pecans (optional)
- 1/4 cup dried cranberries (optional)
- 1/4 cup shredded coconut (for rolling, optional)

DIRECTIONS

Mix ingredients: In a large bowl, combine rolled oats, almond flour, pumpkin puree, almond butter, maple syrup, pumpkin spice mix, and vanilla extract. Mix until well combined.

Add optional ingredients: If using, fold in chopped pecans and dried cranberries.

Form balls: Scoop out small portions of the mixture and roll into balls using your hands.

Roll in coconut: Roll each ball in shredded coconut if desired.

Chill: Place the energy balls in the refrigerator for at least 30 minutes to firm up.

Serve: Enjoy your nutritious and delicious Pumpkin Spice Energy Balls.

Topping variations: Roll in crushed nuts, cocoa powder, or chia seeds for extra flavor and nutrition.

Per serving: 210 calories, 6g protein, 12g fats, 24g carbs

Berry Nutty Snack Mix

Prep. time: 5 min | Cook time: 0 min | Serves: 2

INGREDIENTS

- 1/2 cup almonds
- 1/2 cup cashews
- 1/4 cup dried cranberries
- 1/4 cup dried blueberries
- 2 tbsp pumpkin seeds
- 2 tbsp sunflower seeds
- 1 tbsp chia seeds
- 1 tbsp shredded coconut
- 1 tbsp cacao nibs (optional)
- 1/4 tsp sea salt (optional)

DIRECTIONS

Combine ingredients: In a large bowl, mix together almonds, cashews, dried cranberries, dried blueberries, pumpkin seeds, sunflower seeds, chia seeds, shredded coconut, and cacao nibs (if using).
Mix well: Stir until all ingredients are evenly distributed.
Serve: Divide into two servings and enjoy your nutritious and delicious Berry Nutty Snack Mix.

Topping variations: Add dark chocolate chips, goji berries, or dried mango pieces for extra flavor and nutrition.

Per serving: 280 calories, 8g protein, 20g fats, 22g carbs

Almond Coconut Protein Bars

Prep. time: 10 min | Cook time: 0 min | Serves: 2

INGREDIENTS

- 1/2 cup almonds
- 1/4 cup shredded coconut
- 1/4 cup almond butter
- 1/4 cup protein powder (plant-based)
- 2 tbsp maple syrup
- 1/2 tsp vanilla extract
- 1/8 tsp salt
- 2 tbsp chia seeds
- 2 tbsp coconut oil, melted
- 1/4 cup dark chocolate chips (optional)

DIRECTIONS

Blend ingredients: In a food processor, combine almonds, shredded coconut, almond butter, protein powder, maple syrup, vanilla extract, salt, chia seeds, and melted coconut oil. Blend until well combined.
Add chocolate chips: If using, fold in dark chocolate chips.
Press into pan: Press the mixture evenly into a lined loaf pan.
Chill: Refrigerate for at least 30 minutes until firm.
Cut and serve: Cut into bars and enjoy your nutritious and delicious Almond Coconut Protein Bars.

Toppings variations: Drizzle with additional melted chocolate, or add a handful of dried cranberries for extra flavor and nutrition.

Per serving: 300 calories, 12g protein, 20g fats, 20g carbs

Fresh Veggie Spring Rolls

INGREDIENTS

Prep. time: 15 min   Cook time: 10 min   Serves: 2

- 4 rice paper wrappers
- 1 cup julienned carrots
- 1 cup julienned cucumber
- 1 cup shredded purple cabbage
- 1 avocado, sliced
- 1/2 cup fresh mint leaves
- 1/2 cup fresh cilantro leaves
- 1/2 cup cooked rice noodles
- 1/4 cup chopped peanuts (optional)
- 1/4 cup soy sauce (for dipping, optional)

DIRECTIONS

Prepare spring rolls: Dip a rice paper wrapper in warm water for a few seconds until pliable. Place on a flat surface and layer with carrots, cucumber, cabbage, avocado, mint, cilantro, and rice noodles.
Roll: Fold the sides of the wrapper over the filling and roll tightly. Repeat with remaining wrappers and fillings.
Serve: Serve the spring rolls with soy sauce or your favorite dipping sauce.
Optional toppings: Sprinkle with chopped peanuts for added crunch and flavor.

Topping variations: Add sliced radishes, sprouts, or bell peppers for extra crunch and nutrition.

Per serving: 250 calories, 5g protein, 10g fats, 35g carbs

Mini Stuffed Mushrooms with Spinach and Pine Nuts

INGREDIENTS

Prep. time: 10 min   Cook time: 20 min   Serves: 2

- 12 button mushrooms, stems removed
- 1 cup fresh spinach, chopped
- 2 tbsp pine nuts
- 2 tbsp olive oil
- 1 small onion, finely chopped
- 2 cloves garlic, minced
- 1/4 cup breadcrumbs
- 1 tbsp nutritional yeast (optional)
- Salt and pepper to taste
- 1 tbsp fresh parsley, chopped (optional)

DIRECTIONS

Preheat oven: Preheat your oven to 375°F (190°C) and line a baking sheet with parchment paper.
Cook filling: In a pan, heat 1 tbsp olive oil over medium heat. Sauté onion and garlic until soft. Add chopped spinach and cook until wilted. Stir in pine nuts, breadcrumbs, nutritional yeast, salt, and pepper.
Stuff mushrooms: Fill each mushroom cap with the spinach mixture and place on the prepared baking sheet. Drizzle with remaining olive oil.
Bake: Bake for 15-20 minutes, until mushrooms are tender and the tops are golden.
Serve: Garnish with fresh parsley if desired and serve warm.
Optional toppings: Add a sprinkle of vegan cheese, a drizzle of balsamic glaze, a dusting of smoked paprika, or a squeeze of lemon juice for extra flavor and nutrition.

Topping variations: Add chopped sun-dried tomatoes, a sprinkle of hemp seeds, or a few capers for added texture and taste.

Per serving: 150 calories, 4g protein, 12g fats, 8g carbs

Crispy Cauliflower Bites

Prep. time: 10 min   Cook time: 25 min   Serves: 2

INGREDIENTS

- 1 small head cauliflower, cut into florets
- 1/2 cup chickpea flour
- 1/2 cup water
- 1/2 tsp garlic powder
- 1/2 tsp smoked paprika
- 1/2 tsp salt
- 1 tbsp olive oil
- 1 tbsp chopped fresh parsley (optional)

DIRECTIONS

Preheat oven: Preheat your oven to 425°F (220°C) and line a baking sheet with parchment paper.
Prepare batter: In a bowl, whisk together chickpea flour, water, garlic powder, smoked paprika, and salt until smooth.
Coat cauliflower: Dip each cauliflower floret into the batter, letting excess drip off, and place on the prepared baking sheet.
Bake: Bake for 20-25 minutes until golden and crispy, flipping halfway through.
Serve: Drizzle with olive oil and garnish with chopped fresh parsley if desired.
Optional toppings: Serve with vegan ranch dressing, celery sticks, a sprinkle of nutritional yeast, sliced green onions, or a squeeze of lemon juice for extra flavor and nutrition.

Topping variations: Add chopped chives, sesame seeds, crushed red pepper flakes, or a dollop of guacamole.

Per serving: 160 calories, 5g protein, 7g fats, 20g carbs

Sweet Potato and Avocado Bites

Prep. time: 10 min   Cook time: 20 min   Serves: 2

INGREDIENTS

- 1 large sweet potato, sliced into rounds
- 1 ripe avocado, mashed
- 1 tbsp olive oil
- 1/2 tsp garlic powder
- 1/2 tsp smoked paprika
- 1/4 tsp salt
- 1/4 tsp black pepper
- 1 tbsp lime juice
- 2 tbsp chopped cilantro
- 1 tbsp pumpkin seeds (optional)

DIRECTIONS

Preheat oven: Preheat your oven to 400°F (200°C) and line a baking sheet with parchment paper.
Season sweet potato: In a bowl, toss sweet potato rounds with olive oil, garlic powder, smoked paprika, salt, and black pepper.
Bake: Arrange the sweet potato rounds in a single layer on the baking sheet and bake for 20 minutes, flipping halfway through, until tender and slightly crispy.
Prepare avocado topping: In a small bowl, mix mashed avocado with lime juice and chopped cilantro.
Assemble bites: Top each baked sweet potato round with a spoonful of the avocado mixture.
Serve: Garnish with pumpkin seeds if desired

Topping variations: Add a sprinkle of red pepper flakes, a drizzle of tahini, a dash of hot sauce, sliced cherry tomatoes, hemp seeds, or nutritional yeast for extra flavor and nutrition.

Per serving: 250 calories, 5g protein, 15g fats, 25g carbs

Dips and Spreads
Cilantro Lime White Bean Dip

INGREDIENTS

Prep. time: 10 min   Cook time: 0 min   Serves: 2

- 1 cup cooked white beans
- 1/4 cup fresh cilantro
- 2 tbsp lime juice
- 1 tbsp olive oil
- 1 clove garlic, minced
- 1/2 tsp cumin
- 1/4 tsp salt
- 1/4 tsp black pepper
- 1/4 cup diced red bell pepper (optional)
- 1/4 cup chopped green onions (optional)

DIRECTIONS

Blend ingredients: In a food processor, combine white beans, cilantro, lime juice, olive oil, garlic, cumin, salt, and black pepper. Blend until smooth.
Serve: Transfer the dip to a bowl.
Optional toppings: Garnish with diced red bell pepper and chopped green onions for added flavor and nutrition.

Topping variations: Add avocado slices, cherry tomato halves, or a sprinkle of paprika for extra flavor.

Per serving: 200 calories, 7g protein, 8g fats, 25g carbs

Sweet Potato and Pecan Dip

INGREDIENTS

Prep. time: 10 min   Cook time: 20 min   Serves: 2

- 1 large sweet potato, peeled and cubed
- 1/4 cup pecans, chopped
- 2 tbsp olive oil
- 1 tbsp maple syrup
- 1/2 tsp ground cinnamon
- 1/4 tsp salt
- 1/4 tsp black pepper
- 1/4 cup dried cranberries (optional)
- 1 tbsp chopped parsley (optional)

DIRECTIONS

Cook sweet potato: Boil or steam sweet potato cubes until tender, about 15-20 minutes.
Blend ingredients: In a food processor, combine cooked sweet potato, pecans, olive oil, maple syrup, ground cinnamon, salt, and black pepper. Blend until smooth.
Serve: Transfer the dip to a bowl.
Optional toppings: Garnish with dried cranberries and chopped parsley for added flavor and nutrition.

Topping variations: Add a drizzle of balsamic glaze, a sprinkle of hemp seeds, or a few pomegranate seeds for extra flavor and nutrition.

Per serving: 250 calories, 4g protein, 12g fats, 32g carbs

Classic Creamy Hummus

Prep. time: 10 min	Cook time: 0 min	Serves: 2

INGREDIENTS

- 1 cup cooked chickpeas
- 2 tbsp tahini
- 2 tbsp lemon juice
- 1 clove garlic
- 2 tbsp olive oil
- 1/4 tsp cumin
- 1/4 tsp salt
- 2-3 tbsp water (as needed)
- Paprika (for topping, optional)
- Fresh parsley (for topping, optional)

DIRECTIONS

Blend ingredients: In a food processor, combine chickpeas, tahini, lemon juice, garlic, olive oil, cumin, and salt. Blend until smooth.
Adjust consistency: Add water, 1 tablespoon at a time, until the hummus reaches your desired consistency.
Serve: Transfer the hummus to a bowl.
Optional toppings: Garnish with a sprinkle of paprika and fresh parsley for added flavor and nutrition.

Topping variations: Add a drizzle of extra virgin olive oil, roasted pine nuts, or a few whole chickpeas for extra texture and taste.

Per serving: 220 calories, 6g protein, 14g fats, 18g carbs

Lime Guacamole

Prep. time: 10 min	Cook time: 0 min	Serves: 2

INGREDIENTS

- 2 ripe avocados
- 2 tbsp lime juice
- 1 small tomato, diced
- 1/4 cup red onion, finely chopped
- 2 tbsp fresh cilantro, chopped
- 1 clove garlic, minced
- 1/4 tsp salt
- 1/4 tsp black pepper
- 1/4 tsp cumin (optional)
- 1/4 tsp red pepper flakes (optional)

DIRECTIONS

Mash avocados: In a bowl, mash the avocados with lime juice until smooth.
Mix ingredients: Stir in diced tomato, red onion, cilantro, garlic, salt, black pepper, cumin, and red pepper flakes until well combined.
Serve: Transfer the guacamole to a serving bowl.
Optional toppings: Add extra cilantro, a sprinkle of paprika, or a drizzle of olive oil for added flavor and nutrition.

Topping variations: Garnish with pomegranate seeds, sliced jalapeños, or a dollop of vegan sour cream for extra flavor and texture.

Per serving: 200 calories, 3g protein, 18g fats, 12g carbs

Sun-Dried Tomato and Basil Pesto

INGREDIENTS

Prep. time: 10 min   Cook time: 0 min   Serves: 2

- 1/2 cup sun-dried tomatoes (packed in oil, drained)
- 1 cup fresh basil leaves
- 1/4 cup walnuts
- 1/4 cup nutritional yeast
- 2 cloves garlic
- 2 tbsp lemon juice
- 1/4 cup olive oil
- 1/4 tsp salt
- 1/4 tsp black pepper
- 1/4 cup water (as needed for consistency)

DIRECTIONS

Blend ingredients: In a food processor, combine sun-dried tomatoes, basil leaves, walnuts, nutritional yeast, garlic, lemon juice, olive oil, salt, and black pepper. Blend until smooth, adding water as needed to reach desired consistency.
Serve: Transfer the pesto to a bowl.
Optional toppings: Garnish with extra basil leaves, a sprinkle of nutritional yeast, or chopped walnuts for added flavor and nutrition.

Topping variations: Add a drizzle of balsamic glaze, a few cherry tomato halves, or red pepper flakes for extra flavor and texture.

Per serving: 250 calories, 6g protein, 20g fats, 10g carbs

Garlic and Herb Cashew Cheese Spread

INGREDIENTS

Prep. time: 15 min   Cook time: 0 min   Serves: 2

- 1 cup raw cashews
- 2 tbsp lemon juice
- 2 cloves garlic
- 1/4 cup nutritional yeast
- 2 tbsp olive oil
- 1/4 cup water (more as needed for consistency)
- 1/4 tsp salt
- 1/4 tsp black pepper
- 1 tbsp fresh parsley, chopped
- 1 tbsp fresh chives, chopped

DIRECTIONS

Soak cashews: Soak raw cashews in water for at least 4 hours or overnight, then drain.
Blend ingredients: In a food processor, combine soaked cashews, lemon juice, garlic, nutritional yeast, olive oil, salt, and black pepper. Blend until smooth, adding water as needed to achieve desired consistency.
Mix herbs: Stir in chopped parsley and chives.
Serve: Transfer to a bowl and serve immediately or refrigerate until ready to use.
Optional toppings: Garnish with extra fresh herbs or a drizzle of olive oil for added flavor and nutrition.

Topping variations: Add a sprinkle of smoked paprika, crushed red pepper flakes, or sun-dried tomatoes for extra flavor.

Per serving: 250 calories, 7g protein, 18g fats, 12g carbs

Chapter 8: Salads and Dressings
Green Salads

Classic Caesar Salad with Vegan Parmesan

INGREDIENTS

Prep. time: 10 min   Cook time: 0 min   Serves: 2

- 4 cups romaine lettuce, chopped
- 1/4 cup croutons
- 1/4 cup vegan Parmesan (recipe below)
- 3 tbsp olive oil
- 1 tbsp lemon juice
- 1 tsp Dijon mustard
- 1 clove garlic, minced
- 1/4 tsp salt
- 1/4 tsp black pepper

Vegan Parmesan:

- 1/4 cup raw cashews
- 1 tbsp nutritional yeast
- 1/4 tsp garlic powder
- 1/4 tsp salt

DIRECTIONS

Make vegan Parmesan: In a food processor, blend raw cashews, nutritional yeast, garlic powder, and salt until fine and crumbly.
Prepare dressing: In a bowl, whisk together olive oil, lemon juice, Dijon mustard, minced garlic, salt, and black pepper.
Assemble salad: In a large bowl, combine chopped romaine lettuce, croutons, and vegan Parmesan.
Dress salad: Pour dressing over the salad and toss to coat.
Serve immediately: Enjoy your nutritious and delicious Classic Caesar Salad with Vegan Parmesan.

Optional toppings: Add chickpeas, avocado slices, or cherry tomatoes for extra flavor and nutrition.

Per serving: 220 calories, 5g protein, 16g fats, 14g carbs

Spinach and Strawberry Salad with Poppy Seed Dressing

INGREDIENTS

Prep. time: 10 min   Cook time: 0 min   Serves: 2

- 4 cups fresh spinach
- 1 cup sliced strawberries
- 1/4 cup sliced almonds
- 1/4 cup red onion, thinly sliced
- 2 tbsp poppy seeds
- 2 tbsp olive oil
- 1 tbsp apple cider vinegar
- 1 tbsp maple syrup
- 1/2 tsp Dijon mustard
- Salt and pepper to taste

DIRECTIONS

Prepare dressing: In a small bowl, whisk together olive oil, apple cider vinegar, maple syrup, Dijon mustard, poppy seeds, salt, and pepper.
Assemble salad: In a large bowl, combine spinach, strawberries, sliced almonds, and red onion.
Dress salad: Pour the dressing over the salad and toss gently to coat.
Serve immediately: Enjoy your nutritious and delicious Spinach and Strawberry Salad with Poppy Seed Dressing.

Optional toppings: Add avocado slices or sunflower seeds for extra flavor and nutrition.

Per serving: 200 calories, 5g protein, 14g fats, 18g carbs

Mixed Greens with Avocado and Citrus Vinaigrette

INGREDIENTS

Prep. time: 10 min   Cook time: 0 min   Serves: 2

- 4 cups mixed greens
- 1 avocado, sliced
- 1 orange, segmented
- 1/4 cup red onion, thinly sliced
- 2 tbsp olive oil
- 1 tbsp orange juice
- 1 tbsp lemon juice
- 1 tsp Dijon mustard
- Salt and pepper to taste
- 1 tbsp sunflower seeds (optional)

DIRECTIONS

Prepare dressing: In a small bowl, whisk together olive oil, orange juice, lemon juice, Dijon mustard, salt, and pepper.
Assemble salad: In a large bowl, combine mixed greens, sliced avocado, orange segments, and red onion.
Dress salad: Pour the citrus vinaigrette over the salad and toss gently to coat.
Serve immediately: Enjoy your nutritious and delicious Mixed Greens with Avocado and Citrus Vinaigrette.

Optional toppings: Add sunflower seeds, toasted almonds, or pomegranate seeds for extra flavor and nutrition.

Per serving: 220 calories, 4g protein, 18g fats, 14g carbs

Arugula and Pear Salad with Walnuts and Balsamic Glaze

INGREDIENTS

Prep. time: 10 min   Cook time: 0 min   Serves: 2

DIRECTIONS

- 4 cups arugula
- 1 ripe pear, thinly sliced
- 1/4 cup walnuts, toasted
- 1/4 cup red onion, thinly sliced
- 2 tbsp balsamic glaze
- 2 tbsp olive oil
- 1 tbsp lemon juice
- Salt and pepper to taste

Prepare dressing: In a small bowl, whisk together olive oil, lemon juice, salt, and pepper.
Assemble salad: In a large bowl, combine arugula, sliced pear, toasted walnuts, and red onion.
Dress salad: Pour the dressing over the salad and toss gently to coat.
Drizzle glaze: Drizzle with balsamic glaze just before serving.
Serve immediately: Enjoy your nutritious and delicious Arugula and Pear Salad with Walnuts and Balsamic Glaze.

Optional toppings: Add pomegranate seeds, or sunflower seeds for extra flavor and nutrition.

Per serving: 220 calories, 4g protein, 16g fats, 18g carbs

Cucumber and Mint Salad with Lime Dressing

Prep. time: 10 min   Cook time: 0 min   Serves: 2

INGREDIENTS

- 2 cucumbers, thinly sliced
- 1/4 cup fresh mint leaves, chopped
- 1/4 cup red onion, thinly sliced
- 2 tbsp lime juice
- 1 tbsp olive oil
- 1 tsp maple syrup
- 1/4 tsp salt
- 1/4 tsp black pepper
- 1 tbsp sesame seeds (optional)

DIRECTIONS

Prepare dressing: In a small bowl, whisk together lime juice, olive oil, maple syrup, salt, and black pepper.
Assemble salad: In a large bowl, combine sliced cucumbers, chopped mint leaves, and red onion.
Dress salad: Pour the lime dressing over the salad and toss gently to coat.
Serve immediately: Enjoy your nutritious and delicious Cucumber and Mint Salad with Lime Dressing.

Optional toppings: Add sesame seeds, crushed peanuts, or a sprinkle of chili flakes for extra flavor and nutrition.

Per serving: 120 calories, 2g protein, 8g fats, 10g carbs

Spring Mix Salad with Roasted Beets and Orange Segments

Prep. time: 10 min   Cook time: 30 min   Serves: 2

INGREDIENTS

- 4 cups spring mix greens
- 2 medium beets, roasted and sliced
- 1 orange, segmented
- 1/4 cup red onion, thinly sliced
- 2 tbsp olive oil
- 1 tbsp balsamic vinegar
- 1 tsp maple syrup
- 1/4 tsp salt
- 1/4 tsp black pepper
- 1 tbsp chopped walnuts (optional)

DIRECTIONS

Roast beets: Preheat oven to 400°F (200°C). Wrap beets in foil and roast for 30 minutes or until tender. Let cool, then slice.
Prepare dressing: In a small bowl, whisk together olive oil, balsamic vinegar, maple syrup, salt, and black pepper.
Assemble salad: In a large bowl, combine spring mix greens, roasted beet slices, orange segments, and red onion.
Dress salad: Pour dressing over the salad and toss gently to coat.
Serve immediately: Enjoy your nutritious and delicious Spring Mix Salad with Roasted Beets and Orange Segments.

Optional toppings: Add chopped walnuts, avocado slices, or pomegranate seeds for extra flavor and nutrition.

Per serving: 180 calories, 3g protein, 10g fats, 20g carbs

Kale and Quinoa Salad with Lemon Tahini Dressing

Prep. time: 10 min   Cook time: 0 min   Serves: 2

INGREDIENTS

- 2 cups chopped kale
- 1 cup cooked quinoa
- 1/2 cup cherry tomatoes, halved
- 1/4 cup red onion, thinly sliced
- 1/4 cup shredded carrots
- 2 tbsp sunflower seeds

Lemon Tahini Dressing:

- 2 tbsp tahini
- 2 tbsp lemon juice
- 1 tbsp olive oil
- 1 tbsp maple syrup
- 1 clove garlic, minced
- 1/4 tsp salt
- 2-3 tbsp water (to desired consistency)

DIRECTIONS

Prepare quinoa: Cook quinoa according to package instructions and let cool.
Prepare dressing: In a small bowl, whisk together tahini, lemon juice, olive oil, maple syrup, minced garlic, salt, and water until smooth.
Massage kale: In a large bowl, massage chopped kale with a small amount of the dressing until it begins to soften, about 2-3 minutes.
Assemble salad: Add cooked quinoa, cherry tomatoes, red onion, shredded carrots, and sunflower seeds to the kale.
Dress salad: Pour the lemon tahini dressing over the salad and toss to coat evenly.
Serve immediately: Enjoy your nutritious and delicious Salad.

Optional toppings: Add avocado slices, chickpeas, or cranberries for extra flavor and nutrition.

Per serving: 280 calories, 9g protein, 14g fats, 32g carbs

Brown Rice and Lentil Salad with Lemon Vinaigrette

Prep. time: 10 min   Cook time: 30 min   Serves: 2

INGREDIENTS

- 1 cup cooked brown rice
- 1 cup cooked lentils
- 1/2 cup cherry tomatoes, halved
- 1/4 cup red onion, finely chopped
- 1/2 cup cucumber, diced
- 1/4 cup fresh parsley, chopped
- 2 tbsp sunflower seeds

Lemon Vinaigrette:

- 3 tbsp olive oil
- 2 tbsp lemon juice
- 1 tsp Dijon mustard
- 1 clove garlic, minced
- 1/4 tsp salt
- 1/4 tsp black pepper

DIRECTIONS

Prepare grains and lentils: Cook brown rice and lentils according to package instructions and let cool.
Prepare dressing: In a small bowl, whisk together olive oil, lemon juice, Dijon mustard, minced garlic, salt, and black pepper until well combined.
Assemble salad: In a large bowl, combine cooked brown rice, cooked lentils, cherry tomatoes, red onion, cucumber, parsley, and sunflower seeds.
Dress salad: Pour the lemon vinaigrette over the salad and toss to coat evenly.
Serve immediately: Enjoy your nutritious and delicious Brown Rice and Lentil Salad with Lemon Vinaigrette.

Optional toppings: Add avocado slices, olives, or a sprinkle of nutritional yeast for extra flavor and nutrition.

Per serving: 320 calories, 10g protein, 14g fats, 40g carbs

Grain and Bean Salads

Couscous and Red Bean Salad with Mint and Parsley

Prep. time: 10 min   Cook time: 10 min   Serves: 2

INGREDIENTS

- 1 cup cooked couscous
- 1 cup cooked red beans (rinsed and drained if canned)
- 1/2 cup cherry tomatoes, halved
- 1/4 cup red onion, finely chopped
- 1/4 cup cucumber, diced
- 2 tbsp fresh mint, chopped
- 2 tbsp fresh parsley, chopped
- 2 tbsp olive oil
- 2 tbsp lemon juice
- 1/4 tsp salt
- 1/4 tsp black pepper

DIRECTIONS

Prepare couscous: Cook couscous according to package instructions and let cool.
Mix dressing: In a small bowl, whisk together olive oil, lemon juice, salt, and black pepper.
Assemble salad: In a large bowl, combine cooked couscous, red beans, cherry tomatoes, red onion, cucumber, mint, and parsley.
Dress salad: Pour the dressing over the salad and toss to coat evenly.
Serve immediately: Enjoy your nutritious and delicious Couscous and Red Bean Salad with Mint and Parsley.

Optional toppings: Add avocado slices, toasted almonds, or a sprinkle of feta cheese (if not strictly plant-based) for extra flavor and nutrition.

Per serving: 300 calories, 10g protein, 12g fats, 40g carbs

Quinoa and Black Bean Salad with Avocado Dressing

Prep. time: 10 min   Cook time: 15 min   Serves: 2

INGREDIENTS

- 1 cup cooked quinoa
- 1 cup black beans, rinsed and drained
- 1/2 cup cherry tomatoes, halved
- 1/4 cup red onion, finely chopped
- 1/2 cup corn kernels
- 2 tbsp fresh cilantro, chopped

Avocado Dressing:

- 1 ripe avocado
- 2 tbsp lime juice
- 1 tbsp olive oil
- 1 clove garlic, minced
- 1/4 tsp salt
- 1/4 tsp black pepper
- 2-3 tbsp water

DIRECTIONS

Prepare quinoa: Cook quinoa according to package instructions and let cool.
Prepare dressing: In a blender or food processor, combine avocado, lime juice, olive oil, minced garlic, salt, black pepper, and water. Blend until smooth.
Assemble salad: In a large bowl, combine cooked quinoa, black beans, cherry tomatoes, red onion, corn, and cilantro.
Dress salad: Pour the avocado dressing over the salad and toss gently to coat.
Serve immediately: Enjoy your nutritious and delicious Quinoa and Black Bean Salad with Avocado Dressing.

Optional toppings: Add sliced jalapeños, diced red bell pepper, or a sprinkle of nutritional yeast for extra flavor and nutrition.

Per serving: 350 calories, 12g protein, 16g fats, 40g carbs

Grain and Bean Salads

Millet and Edamame Salad with Ginger Lime Dressing

INGREDIENTS

Prep. time: 10 min   Cook time: 20 min   Serves: 2

- 1 cup cooked millet
- 1 cup shelled edamame, cooked
- 1/2 cup red bell pepper, diced
- 2 tbsp fresh cilantro, chopped
- 2 tbsp sunflower seeds

Ginger Lime Dressing:

- 2 tbsp lime juice
- 1 tbsp olive oil
- 1 tsp fresh ginger, grated
- 1 clove garlic, minced
- 1/4 tsp salt
- 1/4 tsp black pepper

DIRECTIONS

Prepare millet: Cook millet according to package instructions and let cool.
Prepare dressing: In a small bowl, whisk together lime juice, olive oil, grated ginger, minced garlic, salt, and black pepper.
Assemble salad: In a large bowl, combine cooked millet, edamame, red bell pepper, cilantro, and sunflower seeds.
Dress salad: Pour the ginger lime dressing over the salad and toss to coat evenly.
Serve immediately: Enjoy your nutritious and delicious Millet and Edamame Salad with Ginger Lime Dressing.

Optional toppings: Add avocado slices, toasted sesame seeds, or a sprinkle of chili flakes for extra flavor and nutrition.

Per serving: 300 calories, 10g protein, 12g fats, 36g carbs

Barley and White Bean Salad with Pesto

INGREDIENTS

Prep. time: 10 min   Cook time: 30 min   Serves: 2

- 1 cup cooked barley
- 1 cup cooked white beans (rinsed and drained if canned)
- 1/2 cup cherry tomatoes, halved
- 1/4 cup red onion, finely chopped
- 1/4 cup fresh basil leaves, chopped

Pesto:

- 1/2 cup fresh basil leaves
- 2 tbsp olive oil
- 1 tbsp lemon juice
- 1 clove garlic
- 1/4 tsp salt
- 1/4 tsp black pepper

DIRECTIONS

Soak chia seeds: In a small bowl, mix chia seeds with 3 tbsp water and let sit for 5 minutes until gel-like.
Blend smoothie: In a blender, combine chopped beetroot, apple, frozen banana, almond milk, water, soaked chia seeds, lemon juice, and grated ginger. Blend until smooth and creamy.
Serve immediately: Pour the smoothie into two glasses.
Optional toppings: Garnish with hemp seeds and fresh mint leaves for an added boost of flavor and nutrition.

Topping variations: Add fresh berries, or a drizzle of maple syrup for extra flavor and nutrition.

Per serving: 180 calories, 4g protein, 4g fats, 38g carbs

Herbed Chickpea and Tomato Salad

Prep. time: 10 min   Cook time: 0 min   Serves: 2

INGREDIENTS

- 1 cup cooked chickpeas (rinsed and drained if canned)
- 1 cup cherry tomatoes, halved
- 1/4 cup red onion, finely chopped
- 2 tbsp fresh parsley, chopped
- 2 tbsp fresh basil, chopped
- 2 tbsp olive oil
- 1 tbsp lemon juice
- 1 clove garlic, minced
- 1/4 tsp salt
- 1/4 tsp black pepper

DIRECTIONS

Combine ingredients: In a large bowl, combine chickpeas, cherry tomatoes, red onion, parsley, and basil.
Prepare dressing: In a small bowl, whisk together olive oil, lemon juice, minced garlic, salt, and black pepper.
Dress salad: Pour the dressing over the salad and toss gently to coat.
Serve immediately: Enjoy your nutritious and delicious Herbed Chickpea and Tomato Salad.

Optional toppings: Add avocado slices, crumbled vegan feta, or sunflower seeds for extra flavor and nutrition.

Per serving: 220 calories, 6g protein, 14g fats, 18g carbs

Bulgur Wheat and Kidney Bean Herb Salad

Prep. time: 10 min   Cook time: 15 min   Serves: 2

INGREDIENTS

- 1 cup cooked bulgur wheat
- 1 cup cooked kidney beans (rinsed and drained if canned)
- 1/2 cup cherry tomatoes, halved
- 1/4 cup red onion, finely chopped
- 2 tbsp fresh parsley, chopped
- 2 tbsp fresh mint, chopped
- 2 tbsp olive oil
- 2 tbsp lemon juice
- 1 clove garlic, minced
- 1/4 tsp salt
- 1/4 tsp black pepper

DIRECTIONS

Prepare bulgur wheat: Cook bulgur wheat according to package instructions and let cool.
Combine ingredients: In a large bowl, combine cooked bulgur wheat, kidney beans, cherry tomatoes, red onion, parsley, and mint.
Prepare dressing: In a small bowl, whisk together olive oil, lemon juice, minced garlic, salt, and black pepper.
Dress salad: Pour the dressing over the salad and toss gently to coat.
Serve immediately: Enjoy your nutritious and delicious Bulgur Wheat and Kidney Bean Herb Salad.

Optional toppings: Add avocado slices or sunflower seeds for extra flavor and nutrition.

Per serving: 250 calories, 8g protein, 10g fats, 30g carbs

Homemade Dressings

Classic Balsamic Vinaigrette

INGREDIENTS

Prep. time: 5 min   Cook time: 0 min   Serves: 2

- 2 tbsp balsamic vinegar
- 3 tbsp olive oil
- 1 tsp Dijon mustard
- 1 clove garlic, minced
- 1 tsp maple syrup or honey (optional for sweetness)
- 1/4 tsp salt
- 1/4 tsp black pepper

DIRECTIONS

Mix ingredients: In a small bowl, whisk together balsamic vinegar, olive oil, Dijon mustard, minced garlic, maple syrup (if using), salt, and black pepper until well combined.
Serve: Drizzle over salads, roasted vegetables, or use as a marinade and enjoy!

Optional variations: Add a pinch of dried herbs like oregano, thyme, or basil for extra flavor.

Per serving: 130 calories, 1g protein, 14g fats, 2g carbs

Vegan Caesar Dressing

INGREDIENTS

Prep. time: 10 min   Cook time: 0 min   Serves: 2

- 1/4 cup raw cashews (soaked for at least 2 hours)
- 2 tbsp lemon juice
- 1 tbsp Dijon mustard
- 1 tbsp capers
- 1 clove garlic
- 1 tbsp nutritional yeast
- 1 tbsp olive oil
- 1/4 tsp salt
- 1/4 tsp black pepper
- 2-3 tbsp water (to desired consistency)

DIRECTIONS

Soak cashews: Soak raw cashews in water for at least 2 hours, then drain.
Blend ingredients: In a blender or food processor, combine soaked cashews, lemon juice, Dijon mustard, capers, garlic, nutritional yeast, olive oil, salt, and black pepper. Blend until smooth.
Adjust consistency: Add water, 1 tablespoon at a time, until the dressing reaches your desired consistency.
Serve: Drizzle over salads, use as a dip, or enjoy as a spread.

Optional variations: Add a dash of vegan Worcestershire sauce or a pinch of smoked paprika for extra flavor.

Per serving: 160 calories, 5g protein, 12g fats, 10g carbs

Spicy Peanut Dressing

INGREDIENTS

Prep. time: 5 min   Cook time: 0 min   Serves: 2

- 1/4 cup creamy peanut butter
- 2 tbsp soy sauce or tamari
- 1 tbsp lime juice
- 1 tbsp maple syrup
- 1 tbsp rice vinegar
- 1 clove garlic, minced
- 1 tsp fresh ginger, grated
- 1/2 tsp red pepper flakes (adjust to taste)
- 2-3 tbsp water (to desired consistency)

DIRECTIONS

Mix ingredients: In a small bowl, whisk together peanut butter, soy sauce, lime juice, maple syrup, rice vinegar, minced garlic, grated ginger, and red pepper flakes.
Adjust consistency: Add water, 1 tablespoon at a time, until the dressing reaches your desired consistency.
Serve: Drizzle over salads, noodles, or use as a dipping sauce and enjoy!

Optional variations: Add chopped cilantro, a dash of sesame oil, or a sprinkle of crushed peanuts for extra flavor.

Per serving: 140 calories, 5g protein, 10g fats, 8g carbs

Creamy Tahini Dressing

INGREDIENTS

Prep. time: 5 min   Cook time: 0 min   Serves: 2

DIRECTIONS

- 2 tbsp tahini
- 2 tbsp lemon juice
- 1 tbsp olive oil
- 1 tbsp maple syrup
- 1 clove garlic, minced
- 1/4 tsp salt
- 1/4 tsp black pepper
- 2-3 tbsp water (to desired consistency)

Mix ingredients: In a small bowl, whisk together tahini, lemon juice, olive oil, maple syrup, minced garlic, salt, and black pepper until smooth.
Adjust consistency: Add water, 1 tablespoon at a time, until the dressing reaches your desired consistency.
Serve: Drizzle over salads, grain bowls, or use as a dipping sauce and enjoy!

Optional variations: Add a pinch of smoked paprika, cumin, or fresh herbs like parsley or cilantro for extra flavor.

Per serving: 120 calories, 2g protein, 10g fats, 6g carbs

Homemade Dressings

Orange Poppy Seed Dressing

INGREDIENTS

Prep. time: 5 min   Cook time: 0 min   Serves: 2

- 1/4 cup orange juice (freshly squeezed)
- 1 tbsp olive oil
- 1 tbsp apple cider vinegar
- 1 tbsp maple syrup
- 1 tsp poppy seeds
- 1/4 tsp Dijon mustard
- 1/4 tsp salt
- 1/4 tsp black pepper

DIRECTIONS

Mix ingredients: In a small bowl, whisk together orange juice, olive oil, apple cider vinegar, maple syrup, Dijon mustard, salt, and black pepper until well combined.
Add poppy seeds: Stir in the poppy seeds.
Serve: Drizzle over your favorite salad and enjoy!

Optional variations: Add a pinch of orange zest or a bit of minced garlic for extra flavor.

Per serving: 80 calories, 0.5g protein, 7g fats, 5g carbs

Maple Dijon Mustard Dressing

INGREDIENTS

Prep. time: 5 min   Cook time: 0 min   Serves: 2

- 2 tbsp Dijon mustard
- 2 tbsp maple syrup
- 2 tbsp apple cider vinegar
- 1 tbsp olive oil
- 1 clove garlic, minced
- 1/4 tsp salt
- 1/4 tsp black pepper

DIRECTIONS

Mix ingredients: In a small bowl, whisk together Dijon mustard, maple syrup, apple cider vinegar, olive oil, minced garlic, salt, and black pepper until well combined.
Serve: Drizzle over salads or use as a dipping sauce and enjoy!

Optional variations: Add a pinch of red pepper flakes or a squeeze of lemon juice for extra flavor.

Per serving: 100 calories, 1g protein, 7g fats, 10g carbs

Chapter 9: Soups and Stews
Simple Soups

Classic Tomato Basil Soup

INGREDIENTS

Prep. time: 10 min   Cook time: 30 min   Serves: 2

- 4 large tomatoes, chopped
- 1/2 cup onion, finely chopped
- 2 cloves garlic, minced
- 2 cups vegetable broth
- 1/4 cup fresh basil leaves, chopped
- 1 tbsp olive oil
- 1 tsp sugar
- 1/2 tsp salt
- 1/4 tsp black pepper
- 1/4 tsp red pepper flakes (optional)

DIRECTIONS

Cook aromatics: In a large pot, heat olive oil over medium heat. Add chopped onion and minced garlic, and cook until softened, about 5 minutes.

Add tomatoes: Add chopped tomatoes, vegetable broth, sugar, salt, black pepper, and red pepper flakes if using. Bring to a boil, then reduce heat and simmer for 20 minutes.

Blend soup: Use an immersion blender to blend the soup until smooth, or transfer to a blender in batches and blend until smooth.

Add basil: Stir in the chopped basil leaves and simmer for an additional 5 minutes.

Serve: Ladle the soup into bowls and enjoy your nutritious and delicious Classic Tomato Basil Soup.

Optional toppings: Add a drizzle of olive oil, a sprinkle of nutritional yeast, or croutons for extra flavor and texture.

Per serving: 150 calories, 3g protein, 7g fats, 20g carbs

Creamy Coconut Carrot Soup

INGREDIENTS

Prep. time: 10 min   Cook time: 30 min   Serves: 2

- 4 large carrots, peeled and chopped
- 1/2 cup onion, finely chopped
- 2 cloves garlic, minced
- 1 can coconut milk
- 2 cups vegetable broth
- 1 tbsp ginger, grated
- 1 tbsp olive oil
- 1/2 tsp ground cumin
- 1/2 tsp ground coriander
- 1/2 tsp salt
- 1/4 tsp black pepper
- 1 tbsp lime juice
- Fresh cilantro, chopped (optional, for garnish)

DIRECTIONS

Cook aromatics: In a pot, heat olive oil over medium heat. Add onion and garlic; cook until softened, about 5 minutes.

Add ingredients: Add carrots, ginger, cumin, coriander, salt, pepper, and vegetable broth. Simmer for 20 minutes until carrots are tender.

Blend: Blend the soup until smooth using an immersion blender or a regular blender.

Finish: Stir in coconut milk and lime juice, simmer for 5 minutes.

Serve: Ladle into bowls, garnish with cilantro if desired.

Optional toppings: Drizzle with coconut cream, sprinkle red pepper flakes, or add roasted pumpkin seeds.

Per serving: 250 calories, 4g protein, 20g fats, 20g carbs

Simple Soups

Silky Butternut Squash Soup

INGREDIENTS

Prep. time: 10 min   Cook time: 30 min   Serves: 2

- 1 medium butternut squash, peeled, seeded, and cubed
- 1/2 cup onion, chopped
- 2 cloves garlic, minced
- 1 can (14 oz) coconut milk
- 2 cups vegetable broth
- 1 tbsp olive oil
- 1/2 tsp ground nutmeg
- 1/2 tsp ground cinnamon
- 1/2 tsp salt
- 1/4 tsp black pepper
- Fresh thyme leaves (optional, for garnish)

DIRECTIONS

Cook aromatics: In a pot, heat olive oil over medium heat. Add onion and garlic; cook until softened, about 5 minutes.

Add ingredients: Add butternut squash, vegetable broth, nutmeg, cinnamon, salt, and pepper. Simmer for 20 minutes until squash is tender.

Blend: Blend the soup until smooth using an immersion blender or a regular blender.

Finish: Stir in coconut milk, and simmer for 5 minutes.

Serve: Ladle into bowls, garnish with fresh thyme leaves if desired.

Optional toppings: Add a drizzle of coconut cream, a sprinkle of pumpkin seeds, or a dash of smoked paprika for extra flavor.

Per serving: 240 calories, 3g protein, 18g fats, 20g carbs

Ginger Miso Soup with Tofu

INGREDIENTS

Prep. time: 10 min   Cook time: 15 min   Serves: 2

- 4 cups vegetable broth
- 1/2 cup tofu, cubed
- 2 tbsp miso paste
- 1 tbsp fresh ginger, grated
- 2 cloves garlic, minced
- 1 cup baby spinach
- 1/2 cup mushrooms, sliced
- 1 tbsp soy sauce or tamari
- 2 green onions, chopped
- 1 tbsp sesame oil
- 1/4 tsp red pepper flakes (optional)

DIRECTIONS

Cook aromatics: In a pot, heat sesame oil over medium heat. Add ginger and garlic; cook until fragrant, about 2 minutes.

Add broth and tofu: Add vegetable broth, soy sauce, and tofu cubes. Bring to a simmer and cook for 10 minutes.

Add vegetables: Stir in mushrooms and spinach, cooking until the spinach is wilted, about 2-3 minutes.

Mix miso paste: In a small bowl, dissolve miso paste in a little hot broth, then add to the soup.

Serve: Ladle into bowls and garnish with green onions and red pepper flakes if desired.

Optional toppings: Add a sprinkle of sesame seeds, or nori strips for extra flavor and texture.

Per serving: 150 calories, 8g protein, 8g fats, 12g carbs

Lemon Chickpea Orzo Soup

Prep. time: 10 min   Cook time: 20 min   Serves: 2

INGREDIENTS

- 1/2 cup orzo pasta
- 1 cup cooked chickpeas (rinsed and drained if canned)
- 1/2 cup carrots, diced
- 1/2 cup celery, diced
- 1/2 cup onion, chopped
- 4 cups vegetable broth
- 2 tbsp lemon juice
- 1 tbsp olive oil
- 2 cloves garlic, minced
- 1/4 tsp dried thyme
- 1/4 tsp dried oregano
- Salt and pepper to taste
- 2 tbsp fresh parsley, chopped (optional)

DIRECTIONS

Cook aromatics: In a pot, heat olive oil over medium heat. Add onion, carrots, celery, and garlic; cook until softened, about 5 minutes.

Add broth and orzo: Add vegetable broth, orzo, thyme, and oregano. Bring to a boil, then reduce heat and simmer for 10 minutes.

Add chickpeas: Stir in chickpeas and cook until orzo is tender, about 5 more minutes.

Finish: Stir in lemon juice, salt, and pepper to taste.

Serve: Ladle into bowls and garnish with fresh parsley if desired.

Optional toppings: Add a sprinkle of nutritional yeast, a few lemon zest shavings, or a drizzle of extra olive oil for added flavor.

Per serving: 250 calories, 9g protein, 7g fats, 40g carbs

Curried Sweet Potato Soup

Prep. time: 10 min   Cook time: 25 min   Serves: 2

INGREDIENTS

- 2 medium sweet potatoes, peeled and cubed
- 1/2 cup onion, chopped
- 2 cloves garlic, minced
- 1 can (14 oz) coconut milk
- 2 cups vegetable broth
- 1 tbsp olive oil
- 1 tbsp curry powder
- 1 tsp ground ginger
- 1/2 tsp ground cumin
- 1/2 tsp salt
- 1/4 tsp black pepper
- Fresh cilantro, chopped (optional, for garnish)

DIRECTIONS

Cook aromatics: In a pot, heat olive oil over medium heat. Add onion and garlic; cook until softened, about 5 minutes.

Add sweet potatoes and spices: Add cubed sweet potatoes, curry powder, ground ginger, ground cumin, salt, and black pepper. Cook for another 5 minutes, stirring occasionally.

Add liquids: Pour in the vegetable broth and bring to a boil. Reduce heat and simmer for 20 minutes, or until sweet potatoes are tender.

Blend: Use an immersion blender to blend the soup until smooth, or transfer to a blender in batches and blend until smooth.

Finish: Stir in coconut milk and simmer for an additional 5 minutes.

Serve: Ladle into bowls and garnish with fresh cilantro if desired.

Optional toppings: Add a drizzle of coconut cream, a sprinkle of toasted coconut flakes, or a dash of red pepper flakes for extra flavor and texture.

Per serving: 300 calories, 4g protein, 18g fats, 32g carbs

Green Pea and Mint Soup

INGREDIENTS

Prep. time: 10 min   Cook time: 15 min   Serves: 2

- 2 cups frozen green peas
- 1/2 cup onion, chopped
- 2 cloves garlic, minced
- 2 cups vegetable broth
- 1/2 cup coconut milk
- 1 tbsp olive oil
- 1/4 cup fresh mint leaves, chopped
- 1 tbsp lemon juice
- 1/2 tsp salt
- 1/4 tsp black pepper

DIRECTIONS

Cook aromatics: In a pot, heat olive oil over medium heat. Add onion and garlic; cook until softened, about 5 minutes.
Add peas and broth: Add green peas and vegetable broth. Bring to a boil, then reduce heat and simmer for 10 minutes.
Blend: Use an immersion blender to blend the soup until smooth, or transfer to a blender in batches and blend until smooth.
Finish: Stir in coconut milk, chopped mint, lemon juice, salt, and black pepper. Simmer for an additional 2-3 minutes.
Serve: Ladle into bowls and enjoy your nutritious and delicious Green Pea and Mint Soup.

Optional toppings: Add a drizzle of olive oil, a sprinkle of nutritional yeast for extra flavor.

Per serving: 200 calories, 5g protein, 12g fats, 20g carbs

Simple Minestrone Soup

INGREDIENTS

Prep. time: 10 min   Cook time: 30 min   Serves: 2

- 1/2 cup onion, chopped
- 1 clove garlic, minced
- 1/2 cup carrot, diced
- 1/2 cup celery, diced
- 1 cup zucchini, diced
- 1/2 cup canned diced tomatoes
- 1/2 cup canned kidney beans, rinsed and drained
- 1/2 cup small pasta (like ditalini or elbow)
- 4 cups vegetable broth
- 1 tbsp olive oil
- 1 tsp dried oregano
- 1 tsp dried basil
- 1/2 tsp salt
- 1/4 tsp black pepper
- 1/4 cup fresh parsley, chopped (optional)

DIRECTIONS

Cook aromatics: In a pot, heat olive oil over medium heat. Add onion, garlic, carrot, and celery; cook until softened, about 5 minutes.
Add vegetables and broth: Add zucchini, diced tomatoes, kidney beans, vegetable broth, oregano, basil, salt, and black pepper. Bring to a boil.
Add pasta: Add the pasta and reduce heat to a simmer. Cook for 10-15 minutes, until the pasta and vegetables are tender.
Serve: Ladle into bowls and garnish with fresh parsley if desired.

Optional toppings: Add a sprinkle of vegan Parmesan cheese, a drizzle of olive oil, or a pinch of red pepper flakes for extra flavor.

Per serving: 250 calories, 8g protein, 7g fats, 38g carbs

Mushroom and Barley Stew

INGREDIENTS

Prep. time: 10 min   Cook time: 40 min   Serves: 2

- 1 cup mushrooms, sliced
- 1/2 cup pearl barley
- 1/2 cup onion, chopped
- 2 cloves garlic, minced
- 1/2 cup carrots, diced
- 1/2 cup celery, diced
- 4 cups vegetable broth
- 1 tbsp olive oil
- 1 tsp dried thyme
- 1 tsp dried rosemary
- 1/2 tsp salt
- 1/4 tsp black pepper
- 1 tbsp soy sauce or tamari
- 1/4 cup fresh parsley, chopped (optional)

DIRECTIONS

Cook aromatics: In a pot, heat olive oil over medium heat. Add onion, garlic, carrots, and celery; cook until softened, about 5 minutes.

Add mushrooms: Add sliced mushrooms and cook for another 5 minutes until they begin to soften.

Add barley and broth: Stir in the pearl barley, vegetable broth, thyme, rosemary, salt, black pepper, and soy sauce. Bring to a boil.

Simmer: Reduce heat to a simmer and cook for 30-35 minutes, until the barley is tender and the stew has thickened.

Serve: Ladle into bowls and garnish with fresh parsley if desired.

Optional toppings: Add a drizzle of truffle oil, a sprinkle of nutritional yeast, or a dollop of vegan sour cream for extra flavor.

Per serving: 300 calories, 8g protein, 9g fats, 45g carbs

Chunky Vegetable and Bean Stew

INGREDIENTS

Prep. time: 10 min   Cook time: 30 min   Serves: 2

- 1 cup potatoes, diced
- 1/2 cup carrots, sliced
- 1/2 cup celery, diced
- 1/2 cup onion, chopped
- 1 cup canned diced tomatoes
- 1 cup canned white beans, rinsed and drained
- 2 cups vegetable broth
- 1 tbsp olive oil
- 2 cloves garlic, minced
- 1 tsp dried thyme
- 1 tsp dried oregano
- 1/2 tsp smoked paprika
- 1/2 tsp salt
- 1/4 tsp black pepper
- 1/4 cup fresh parsley, chopped (optional)

DIRECTIONS

Cook aromatics: In a pot, heat olive oil over medium heat. Add onion and garlic; cook until softened, about 5 minutes.

Add vegetables: Add potatoes, carrots, and celery. Cook for another 5 minutes, stirring occasionally.

Add liquids and seasonings: Stir in diced tomatoes, vegetable broth, thyme, oregano, smoked paprika, salt, and black pepper. Bring to a boil.

Simmer: Reduce heat to a simmer and cook for 20 minutes, or until vegetables are tender.

Add beans: Stir in white beans and cook for an additional 5 minutes to heat through.

Serve: Ladle into bowls and garnish with fresh parsley if desired.

Optional toppings: Add a drizzle of olive oil or a sprinkle of nutritional yeast for extra flavor and texture.

Per serving: 250 calories, 8g protein, 8g fats, 36g carbs

Hearty Chickpea and Spinach Stew

INGREDIENTS

Prep. time: 10 min   Cook time: 25 min   Serves: 2

- 1 cup canned chickpeas, rinsed and drained
- 2 cups fresh spinach, chopped
- 1/2 cup onion, chopped
- 2 cloves garlic, minced
- 1 cup diced tomatoes (canned or fresh)
- 2 cups vegetable broth
- 1/2 cup carrots, sliced
- 1 tbsp olive oil
- 1 tsp ground cumin
- 1 tsp ground coriander
- 1/2 tsp smoked paprika
- 1/2 tsp salt
- 1/4 tsp black pepper
- 1/4 cup fresh parsley, chopped (optional)

DIRECTIONS

Cook aromatics: In a pot, heat olive oil over medium heat. Add onion and garlic; cook until softened, about 5 minutes.
Add vegetables and spices: Add carrots, cumin, coriander, and smoked paprika. Cook for another 5 minutes, stirring occasionally.
Add liquids and chickpeas: Stir in diced tomatoes, vegetable broth, chickpeas, salt, and black pepper. Bring to a boil.
Simmer: Reduce heat to a simmer and cook for 15 minutes, or until the carrots are tender.
Add spinach: Stir in the chopped spinach and cook for an additional 2-3 minutes until wilted.
Serve: Ladle into bowls and garnish with fresh parsley if desired.

Optional toppings: Add a squeeze of lemon juice, a drizzle of olive oil, or a sprinkle of nutritional yeast for extra flavor.

Per serving: 220 calories, 9g protein, 8g fats, 28g carbs

Lentil and Root Vegetable Stew

INGREDIENTS

Prep. time: 10 min   Cook time: 30 min   Serves: 2

- 1/2 cup dried lentils, rinsed
- 1 cup potatoes, diced
- 1/2 cup carrots, sliced
- 1/2 cup parsnips, diced
- 1/2 cup onion, chopped
- 2 cloves garlic, minced
- 4 cups vegetable broth
- 1 can (14 oz) diced tomatoes
- 1 tbsp olive oil
- 1 tsp dried thyme
- 1 tsp dried rosemary
- 1/2 tsp ground cumin
- 1/2 tsp smoked paprika
- 1/2 tsp salt
- 1/4 tsp black pepper
- 1/4 cup fresh parsley, chopped (optional)

DIRECTIONS

Cook aromatics: In a pot, heat olive oil over medium heat. Add onion and garlic; cook until softened, about 5 minutes.
Add vegetables and spices: Add potatoes, carrots, parsnips, thyme, rosemary, cumin, and smoked paprika. Cook for another 5 minutes, stirring occasionally.
Add liquids and lentils: Stir in diced tomatoes, vegetable broth, lentils, salt, and black pepper. Bring to a boil.
Simmer: Reduce heat to a simmer and cook for 20-25 minutes, or until the lentils and root vegetables are tender.
Serve: Ladle into bowls and garnish with fresh parsley if desired.

Optional toppings: Add a drizzle of balsamic vinegar, a sprinkle of nutritional yeast, or croutons for extra flavor and texture.

Per serving: 300 calories, 15g protein, 8g fats, 45g carbs

Quinoa and Kale Stew

Prep. time: 10 min   Cook time: 25 min   Serves: 2

INGREDIENTS

- 1/2 cup quinoa, rinsed
- 2 cups kale, chopped
- 1/2 cup onion, chopped
- 2 cloves garlic, minced
- 1 cup diced tomatoes (canned or fresh)
- 4 cups vegetable broth
- 1/2 cup carrots, sliced
- 1/2 cup celery, diced
- 1 tbsp olive oil
- 1 tsp dried thyme
- 1 tsp dried oregano
- 1/2 tsp smoked paprika
- 1/2 tsp salt
- 1/4 tsp black pepper
- 1/4 cup fresh parsley, chopped (optional)

DIRECTIONS

Cook aromatics: In a pot, heat olive oil over medium heat. Add onion and garlic; cook until softened, about 5 minutes.

Add vegetables and quinoa: Add carrots, celery, quinoa, thyme, oregano, and smoked paprika. Cook for another 5 minutes, stirring occasionally.

Add liquids: Stir in diced tomatoes, vegetable broth, salt, and black pepper. Bring to a boil.

Simmer: Reduce heat to a simmer and cook for 15 minutes, or until the quinoa is tender.

Add kale: Stir in the chopped kale and cook for an additional 5 minutes until wilted.

Serve: Ladle into bowls and garnish with fresh parsley if desired.

Optional toppings: Add a squeeze of lemon juice, a sprinkle of nutritional yeast, or a few avocado slices for extra flavor and nutrition.

Per serving: 250 calories, 9g protein, 8g fats, 36g carbs

Sweet Potato and Black Bean Stew

Prep. time: 10 min   Cook time: 30 min   Serves: 2

INGREDIENTS

- 1 large sweet potato, peeled and cubed
- 1 cup canned black beans, rinsed and drained
- 1/2 cup onion, chopped
- 2 cloves garlic, minced
- 1 cup diced tomatoes (canned or fresh)
- 2 cups vegetable broth
- 1/2 cup bell pepper, diced
- 1 tbsp olive oil
- 1 tsp ground cumin
- 1 tsp chili powder
- 1/2 tsp smoked paprika
- 1/2 tsp salt
- 1/4 tsp black pepper
- 1/4 cup fresh cilantro, chopped (optional)

DIRECTIONS

Cook aromatics: In a pot, heat olive oil over medium heat. Add onion and garlic; cook until softened, about 5 minutes.

Add vegetables and spices: Add sweet potato, bell pepper, cumin, chili powder, and smoked paprika. Cook for another 5 minutes, stirring occasionally.

Add liquids and beans: Stir in diced tomatoes, vegetable broth, black beans, salt, and black pepper. Bring to a boil.

Simmer: Reduce heat to a simmer and cook for 20-25 minutes, or until the sweet potatoes are tender.

Serve: Ladle into bowls and garnish with fresh cilantro if desired.

Optional toppings: Add a squeeze of lime juice, a dollop of vegan sour cream, or avocado slices for extra flavor and nutrition.

Per serving: 280 calories, 9g protein, 8g fats, 46g carbs

Curried Cauliflower and Potato Stew

Prep. time: 10 min   Cook time: 25 min   Serves: 2

INGREDIENTS

- 1 cup cauliflower florets
- 1 large potato, peeled and cubed
- 1/2 cup onion, chopped
- 2 cloves garlic, minced
- 1 can (14 oz) diced tomatoes
- 2 cups vegetable broth
- 1/2 cup coconut milk
- 1 tbsp olive oil
- 1 tbsp curry powder
- 1 tsp ground cumin
- 1/2 tsp ground turmeric
- 1/2 tsp salt
- 1/4 tsp black pepper
- 1/4 cup fresh cilantro, chopped (optional)

DIRECTIONS

Cook aromatics: In a pot, heat olive oil over medium heat. Add onion and garlic; cook until softened, about 5 minutes.
Add spices: Stir in curry powder, ground cumin, and ground turmeric; cook for 1-2 minutes until fragrant.
Add vegetables: Add cauliflower florets and cubed potato; cook for another 5 minutes, stirring occasionally.
Add liquids: Stir in diced tomatoes, vegetable broth, coconut milk, salt, and black pepper. Bring to a boil.
Simmer: Reduce heat to a simmer and cook for 20 minutes, or until the potatoes and cauliflower are tender.
Serve: Ladle into bowls and garnish with fresh cilantro if desired.

Optional toppings: Add a squeeze of lime juice, a dollop of vegan yogurt, or a sprinkle of red pepper flakes for extra flavor and texture.

Per serving: 300 calories, 7g protein, 15g fats, 35g carbs

Savory Tofu and Cabbage Stew

Prep. time: 10 min   Cook time: 25 min   Serves: 2

INGREDIENTS

- 1 cup tofu, cubed
- 2 cups green cabbage, chopped
- 1/2 cup onion, chopped
- 2 cloves garlic, minced
- 1 cup carrots, sliced
- 2 cups vegetable broth
- 1 can (14 oz) diced tomatoes
- 1 tbsp soy sauce or tamari
- 1 tbsp olive oil
- 1 tsp dried thyme
- 1/2 tsp smoked paprika
- 1/2 tsp salt
- 1/4 tsp black pepper
- 1/4 cup fresh parsley, chopped (optional)

DIRECTIONS

Cook tofu: In a pot, heat olive oil over medium heat. Add cubed tofu and cook until lightly browned, about 5 minutes. Remove tofu from pot and set aside.
Cook aromatics: In the same pot, add onion and garlic; cook until softened, about 5 minutes.
Add vegetables and spices: Add chopped cabbage, sliced carrots, thyme, and smoked paprika. Cook for another 5 minutes, stirring occasionally.
Add liquids: Stir in diced tomatoes, vegetable broth, soy sauce, salt, and black pepper. Bring to a boil.
Simmer: Reduce heat to a simmer and cook for 15 minutes, or until the vegetables are tender.
Add tofu: Return the tofu to the pot and cook for an additional 5 minutes to heat through.
Serve: Ladle into bowls and garnish with fresh parsley if desired.

Optional toppings: Add a squeeze of lemon juice, a sprinkle of nutritional yeast, or a dash of hot sauce for extra flavor.

Per serving: 250 calories, 12g protein, 10g fats, 28g carbs

Chapter 10: Main Dishes
Pasta and Noodles

Spaghetti with Lentil Bolognese

INGREDIENTS

Prep. time: 10 min   Cook time: 30 min   Serves: 2

- 4 oz spaghetti (whole grain or gluten-free if desired)
- 1 cup cooked lentils (rinsed and drained if canned)
- 1/2 cup onion, chopped
- 2 cloves garlic, minced
- 1 can (14 oz) diced tomatoes
- 2 tbsp tomato paste
- 1 tbsp olive oil
- 1 tsp dried oregano
- 1/2 tsp salt
- 1/4 tsp black pepper

DIRECTIONS

Cook spaghetti: Cook spaghetti according to package instructions. Drain and set aside.
Cook aromatics: In a large pot, heat olive oil over medium heat. Add onion and garlic; cook until softened, about 5 minutes.
Add lentils and tomatoes: Stir in cooked lentils, diced tomatoes, tomato paste, oregano, salt, and black pepper. Bring to a simmer and cook for 15-20 minutes, until the sauce thickens.
Combine: Serve the lentil Bolognese sauce over the cooked spaghetti.

Optional toppings: Add fresh parsley, nutritional yeast, or a sprinkle of red pepper flakes for extra flavor.

Per serving: 350 calories, 14g protein, 9g fats, 55g carbs

Peanut Sauce Noodles with Tofu

INGREDIENTS

Prep. time: 10 min   Cook time: 15 min   Serves: 2

- 4 oz rice noodles or your choice of noodles
- 1 cup tofu, cubed
- 1/2 cup bell pepper, sliced
- 1 tbsp olive oil

Peanut Sauce:

- 1/4 cup creamy peanut butter
- 2 tbsp soy sauce or tamari
- 1 tbsp lime juice
- 1 tbsp maple syrup
- 2-3 tbsp water (to desired consistency)

DIRECTIONS

Prepare noodles: Cook noodles according to package instructions. Drain and set aside.
Cook tofu: In a large pan, heat olive oil over medium heat. Add cubed tofu and cook until golden brown on all sides, about 5-7 minutes. Remove tofu from pan and set aside.
Cook bell pepper: In the same pan, add sliced bell pepper and cook until tender, about 3-5 minutes.
Make peanut sauce: In a small bowl, whisk together peanut butter, soy sauce, lime juice, maple syrup, and water until smooth.
Combine: Add cooked noodles, tofu, and peanut sauce to the pan with bell pepper. Toss to coat everything evenly.
Serve: Garnish with additional toppings if desired.

Optional toppings: Add crushed peanuts, sesame seeds, or a sprinkle of red pepper flakes for extra flavor and texture.

Per serving: 350 calories, 14g protein, 16g fats, 40g carbs

Lemon Garlic Pasta with Asparagus

INGREDIENTS

- 4 oz pasta (your choice)
- 1 cup asparagus, trimmed and cut into 1-inch pieces
- 2 cloves garlic, minced
- 2 tbsp olive oil
- 1 tbsp lemon juice
- 1 tsp lemon zest
- Salt and pepper to taste
- 1/4 cup fresh parsley, chopped (optional)

DIRECTIONS

Cook pasta: Cook pasta according to package instructions. Drain and set aside.
Cook asparagus: In a large pan, heat 1 tbsp olive oil over medium heat. Add asparagus and cook until tender, about 5 minutes. Remove asparagus from pan and set aside.
Cook garlic: In the same pan, add the remaining olive oil and minced garlic. Cook until fragrant, about 1-2 minutes.
Combine ingredients: Add cooked pasta, asparagus, lemon juice, and lemon zest to the pan. Toss to coat everything evenly. Season with salt and pepper to taste.
Serve: Garnish with fresh parsley if desired.

Optional toppings: Add a sprinkle of nutritional yeast, red pepper flakes, or vegan Parmesan for extra flavor.

Per serving: 300 calories, 8g protein, 12g fats, 40g carbs

Pasta Primavera with Cashew Cream Sauce

Prep. time: 15 min   Cook time: 20 min   Serves: 2

INGREDIENTS

- 4 oz pasta (your choice)
- 1 cup mixed vegetables (e.g., bell peppers, zucchini, cherry tomatoes, broccoli)
- 1/2 cup raw cashews (soaked for at least 2 hours)
- 1/2 cup water
- 2 cloves garlic, minced
- 2 tbsp olive oil
- 2 tbsp lemon juice
- 1/2 tsp salt
- 1/4 tsp black pepper
- 1/4 cup fresh basil, chopped (optional)

DIRECTIONS

Prepare cashew cream: Drain soaked cashews. In a blender, combine cashews, water, lemon juice, salt, and black pepper. Blend until smooth.
Cook pasta: Cook pasta according to package instructions. Drain and set aside.
Cook vegetables: In a large pan, heat olive oil over medium heat. Add minced garlic and cook until fragrant, about 1 minute. Add mixed vegetables and cook until tender, about 5-7 minutes.
Combine ingredients: Add cooked pasta and cashew cream sauce to the pan with the vegetables. Toss to coat everything evenly.
Serve: Garnish with fresh basil if desired.

Optional toppings: Add a sprinkle of nutritional yeast, red pepper flakes, or vegan Parmesan for extra flavor.

Per serving: 350 calories, 10g protein, 18g fats, 40g carbs

Spicy Sesame Soba Noodles

INGREDIENTS

Prep. time: 10 min   Cook time: 10 min   Serves: 2

- 4 oz soba noodles
- 1/2 cup bell pepper, julienned
- 1/2 cup carrots, julienned
- 1/4 cup green onions, chopped
- 2 tbsp soy sauce or tamari
- 1 tbsp sesame oil
- 1 tbsp rice vinegar
- 1 tbsp maple syrup
- 1 clove garlic, minced
- 1 tsp fresh ginger, grated
- 1 tsp red pepper flakes (adjust to taste)
- 1 tbsp sesame seeds

DIRECTIONS

Cook noodles: Cook soba noodles according to package instructions. Drain and rinse under cold water.
Prepare sauce: In a small bowl, whisk together soy sauce, sesame oil, rice vinegar, maple syrup, minced garlic, grated ginger, and red pepper flakes.
Combine ingredients: In a large bowl, toss cooked soba noodles with bell pepper, carrots, green onions, and the prepared sauce until evenly coated.
Serve: Sprinkle with sesame seeds and enjoy your Spicy Sesame Soba Noodles.

Optional toppings: Add avocado slices, crushed peanuts, or a squeeze of lime for extra flavor and texture.

Per serving: 300 calories, 8g protein, 10g fats, 45g carbs

Vegan Pesto Pasta with Cherry Tomatoes

INGREDIENTS

Prep. time: 5 min   Cook time: 0 min   Serves: 2

- 4 oz pasta (your choice)
- 1 cup cherry tomatoes, halved
- 2 cups fresh basil leaves
- 1/4 cup pine nuts or walnuts
- 2 cloves garlic
- 1/4 cup nutritional yeast
- 1/4 cup olive oil
- 1 tbsp lemon juice
- Salt and pepper to taste

DIRECTIONS

Cook pasta: Cook pasta according to package instructions. Drain and set aside.
Make pesto: In a food processor, combine basil leaves, pine nuts or walnuts, garlic, nutritional yeast, lemon juice, salt, and pepper. Pulse until finely chopped. With the processor running, slowly add olive oil until the mixture is smooth and creamy.
Combine ingredients: In a large bowl, toss the cooked pasta with the pesto until evenly coated. Add the cherry tomatoes and toss gently to combine.
Serve: Divide into bowls and enjoy your Vegan Pesto Pasta with Cherry Tomatoes.

Optional toppings: Add a sprinkle of red pepper flakes, vegan Parmesan, or a handful of arugula for extra flavor and texture.

Per serving: 350 calories, 10g protein, 20g fats, 35g carbs

Creamy Potato Gratin

INGREDIENTS

Prep. time: 15 min   Cook time: 45 min   Serves: 4

- 4 large potatoes, thinly sliced
- 2 cups unsweetened almond milk or other plant-based milk
- 1 cup coconut cream or cashew cream
- 4 cloves garlic, minced
- 1 cup nutritional yeast
- 4 tbsp olive oil
- 2 tsp dried thyme
- 1 tsp salt
- 1/2 tsp black pepper
- 1/4 cup fresh parsley, chopped (optional, for garnish)

DIRECTIONS

Preheat oven: Preheat to 375°F (190°C).
Prepare sauce: Heat olive oil in a saucepan, cook garlic for 1-2 minutes. Add almond milk, coconut cream, nutritional yeast, thyme, salt, and pepper. Cook until thickened, about 5 minutes.
Assemble gratin: Layer half the potatoes in a baking dish, pour half the sauce over. Repeat with remaining potatoes and sauce.
Bake: Cover with foil and bake for 30 minutes. Remove foil and bake for an additional 15 minutes, until tender and golden brown.
Serve: Let cool before serving. Garnish with parsley if desired.

Optional toppings: Add vegan Parmesan or breadcrumbs for extra texture.

Per serving: 300 calories, 7g protein, 18g fats, 30g carbs

Classic Vegetable Lasagna

INGREDIENTS

Prep. time: 20 min   Cook time: 45 min   Serves: 4

- 9 lasagna noodles
- 2 cups marinara sauce
- 2 cups ricotta (use cashew or tofu ricotta for a vegan version)
- 1 cup shredded mozzarella (use vegan mozzarella for a vegan version)
- 1 cup zucchini, sliced
- 1 cup mushrooms, sliced
- 1 cup spinach, chopped
- 1/2 cup onion, chopped
- 2 cloves garlic, minced
- 2 tbsp olive oil
- 1 tsp dried oregano
- 1 tsp dried basil
- 1/2 tsp salt
- 1/4 tsp black pepper

DIRECTIONS

Preheat oven: Preheat to 375°F (190°C).
Cook noodles: Cook lasagna noodles according to package instructions. Drain and set aside.
Cook vegetables: In a pan, heat olive oil over medium heat. Add onion, garlic, zucchini, mushrooms, spinach, oregano, basil, salt, and pepper. Cook until tender, about 5 minutes.
Assemble lasagna: Spread a thin layer of marinara sauce in a baking dish. Layer with 3 noodles, half of the ricotta, half of the vegetable mixture, and a third of the mozzarella. Repeat layers, finishing with noodles, marinara sauce, and remaining mozzarella.
Bake: Cover with foil and bake for 30 minutes. Remove foil and bake for 15 minutes more, until the top is golden and bubbly.
Serve: Let cool before slicing and serving.

Optional toppings: Garnish with fresh basil or parsley.

Per serving: 400 calories, 18g protein, 15g fats, 50g carbs

Mushroom and Wild Rice Casserole

INGREDIENTS

Prep. time: 15 min   Cook time: 45 min   Serves: 4

- 1 cup wild rice, rinsed and drained
- 2 cups vegetable broth
- 2 cups mushrooms, sliced
- 1 cup broccoli florets
- 1/2 cup onion, chopped
- 2 cloves garlic, minced
- 1 cup unsweetened almond milk or other plant-based milk
- 1/2 cup nutritional yeast
- 2 tbsp olive oil
- 1 tbsp flour (use gluten-free)
- 1 tsp dried thyme
- 1/2 tsp salt
- 1/4 tsp black pepper

DIRECTIONS

Cook rice: In a pot, combine wild rice and vegetable broth. Simmer for 30-35 minutes until tender.

Cook vegetables: In a pan, heat olive oil over medium heat. Sauté onion, garlic, and mushrooms for 5 minutes. Add broccoli and cook 5 more minutes.

Make sauce: Sprinkle flour over vegetables. Gradually add almond milk, stirring until thickened. Add nutritional yeast, thyme, salt, and pepper.

Combine and bake: Preheat oven to 375°F (190°C). Mix cooked rice and vegetables in a baking dish. Cover with foil and bake for 20 minutes. Remove foil and bake 10 more minutes until golden.

Serve: Let cool slightly before serving.

Optional toppings: Add parsley, crushed almonds, or vegan cheese for extra flavor.

Per serving: 300 calories, 10g protein, 12g fats, 40g carbs

Butternut Squash and Spinach Casserole

INGREDIENTS

Prep. time: 15 min   Cook time: 40 min   Serves: 4

DIRECTIONS

- 4 cups butternut squash, peeled and cubed
- 2 cups fresh spinach, chopped
- 1/2 cup onion, chopped
- 2 cloves garlic, minced
- 1 cup unsweetened almond milk or other plant-based milk
- 1/2 cup nutritional yeast
- 2 tbsp olive oil
- 1 tbsp flour (use gluten-free if needed)
- 1 tsp dried thyme
- 1/2 tsp salt
- 1/4 tsp black pepper
- 1/4 cup breadcrumbs (use gluten-free if needed)

Preheat oven: Preheat to 375°F (190°C).

Cook squash: Steam or boil butternut squash until tender, about 10 minutes.

Cook aromatics: In a pan, heat olive oil. Sauté onion and garlic until softened, about 5 minutes.

Make sauce: Sprinkle flour over onions and garlic, stir. Gradually add almond milk, stirring until thickened. Add nutritional yeast, thyme, salt, and pepper.

Assemble casserole: In a baking dish, combine cooked squash and spinach. Pour sauce over and mix well.

Add topping: Sprinkle breadcrumbs evenly on top.

Bake: Cover with foil and bake for 20 minutes. Remove foil and bake for 10 more minutes until golden.

Serve: Let cool slightly before serving.

Optional toppings: Add vegan cheese, chopped nuts, or fresh herbs for extra flavor.

Per serving: 250 calories, 8g protein, 10g fats, 35g carbs

Casseroles# Casseroles and Bakes

Sweet Potato and Kale Gratin

Prep. time: 15 min   Cook time: 40 min   Serves: 4

INGREDIENTS

- 2 large sweet potatoes, peeled and thinly sliced
- 2 cups kale, chopped and stems removed
- 1 cup unsweetened almond milk or other plant-based milk
- 1/2 cup nutritional yeast
- 1/2 cup coconut cream or cashew cream
- 2 cloves garlic, minced
- 2 tbsp olive oil
- 1 tbsp flour (use gluten-free if needed)
- 1 tsp dried thyme
- 1/2 tsp salt
- 1/4 tsp black pepper
- 1/4 cup breadcrumbs (optional, use gluten-free)

DIRECTIONS

Preheat oven: Preheat to 375°F (190°C).
Prepare sauce: In a saucepan, heat olive oil. Add garlic and cook for 1-2 minutes. Stir in flour. Gradually add almond milk, stirring until thickened. Add nutritional yeast, coconut cream, thyme, salt, and pepper.
Assemble gratin: In a baking dish, layer half the sweet potatoes, top with half the kale, and pour half the sauce. Repeat layers.
Add topping: Sprinkle breadcrumbs on top if using.
Bake: Cover with foil and bake for 25 minutes. Remove foil and bake for another 15 minutes until golden.
Serve: Let cool slightly before serving.

Optional toppings: Add vegan cheese or chopped nuts for extra flavor.

Per serving: 280 calories, 6g protein, 14g fats, 32g carbs

Mexican Black Bean and Corn Bake

Prep. time: 10 min   Cook time: 30 min   Serves: 2

INGREDIENTS

- 1 can (15 oz) black beans, rinsed and drained
- 1 cup corn kernels (fresh or frozen)
- 1 cup salsa
- 1/2 cup diced bell pepper
- 1/2 cup diced onion
- 1 cup cooked quinoa or rice
- 1/2 cup shredded vegan cheese (optional)
- 1 tsp ground cumin
- 1 tsp chili powder
- 1/2 tsp garlic powder
- 1/2 tsp salt
- 1/4 tsp black pepper
- 2 tbsp chopped fresh cilantro (optional, for garnish)

DIRECTIONS

Preheat oven: Preheat to 375°F (190°C).
Mix ingredients: In a large bowl, combine black beans, corn, salsa, bell pepper, onion, cooked quinoa or rice, cumin, chili powder, garlic powder, salt, and pepper.
Assemble bake: Transfer the mixture to a baking dish. Top with shredded vegan cheese if using.
Bake: Bake for 20-25 minutes, until heated through and the cheese is melted.
Serve: Garnish with fresh cilantro if desired.

Optional toppings: Add avocado slices, a dollop of vegan sour cream, or a squeeze of lime juice for extra flavor.

Per serving: 250 calories, 10g protein, 6g fats, 40g carbs

Grilled Veggie and Hummus Wraps

INGREDIENTS

Prep. time: 10 min   Cook time: 15 min   Serves: 2

- 1 zucchini, sliced
- 1 red bell pepper, sliced
- 1/2 red onion, sliced
- 1 tbsp olive oil
- 1/2 tsp salt
- 1/4 tsp black pepper
- 4 large tortillas or wraps
- 1/2 cup hummus
- 1/4 cup chopped fresh parsley (optional)

DIRECTIONS

Preheat grill: Preheat grill or grill pan over medium-high heat.
Grill veggies: Toss zucchini, bell pepper, and red onion with olive oil, salt, and pepper. Grill vegetables for about 5-7 minutes on each side until tender and slightly charred.
Warm tortillas: Heat tortillas in a dry pan over medium heat for about 30 seconds on each side until warm and pliable.
Assemble wraps: Spread a layer of hummus on each tortilla. Add a portion of the grilled vegetables.
Serve: Roll up the tortillas and enjoy immediately. Garnish with chopped fresh parsley if desired.

Optional toppings: Add a sprinkle of red pepper flakes, a squeeze of lemon juice, or a drizzle of balsamic glaze for extra flavor.

Per serving: 250 calories, 7g protein, 11g fats, 30g carbs

Spicy Lentil Tacos

INGREDIENTS

Prep. time: 10 min   Cook time: 20 min   Serves: 2

- 1/2 cup dried lentils, rinsed
- 1 cup vegetable broth or water
- 1/2 cup diced onion
- 1 tsp olive oil
- 1 tsp ground cumin
- 1 tsp chili powder
- Salt and pepper to taste
- 4 small corn tortillas
- 1/2 cup diced tomatoes
- 1/2 avocado, sliced (optional)
- Lime wedges for serving (optional)

DIRECTIONS

Cook lentils: In a pot, combine lentils and vegetable broth. Bring to a boil, reduce heat, cover, and simmer for 15-20 minutes until lentils are tender and liquid is absorbed.
Cook aromatics: In a pan, heat olive oil over medium heat. Add diced onion and cook until softened, about 5 minutes.
Add spices and lentils: Stir in cooked lentils, cumin, chili powder, salt, and pepper. Cook for another 5 minutes, stirring occasionally.
Warm tortillas: Heat tortillas in a dry pan over medium heat for about 30 seconds on each side until warm and pliable.
Assemble tacos: Divide lentil mixture among the tortillas. Top with diced tomatoes and avocado slices if desired.
Serve: Squeeze lime wedges over the tacos if desired.

Optional toppings: Add a drizzle of hot sauce or vegan sour cream for extra flavor.

Per serving: 250 calories, 10g protein, 8g fats, 35g carbs

Thai Peanut Tofu Wraps

INGREDIENTS

Prep. time: 10 min   Cook time: 10 min   Serves: 2

- 1 cup tofu, cubed
- 1/2 cup shredded carrots
- 1/2 cup shredded cabbage
- 1/4 cup chopped cilantro
- 2 large tortillas or wraps
- 1/4 cup peanut sauce
- 1 tbsp olive oil
- Salt to taste

DIRECTIONS

Cook tofu: In a pan, heat olive oil over medium heat. Add cubed tofu and cook until golden brown on all sides, about 5-7 minutes. Season with salt.

Prepare vegetables: In a bowl, mix shredded carrots, shredded cabbage, and chopped cilantro.

Warm tortillas: Heat tortillas in a dry pan over medium heat for about 30 seconds on each side until warm and pliable.

Assemble wraps: Spread a layer of peanut sauce on each tortilla. Add a portion of the cooked tofu and top with the vegetable mixture.

Serve: Wrap up the tortillas and enjoy immediately.

Optional toppings: Add a sprinkle of chopped peanuts, a squeeze of lime juice, or red pepper flakes for extra flavor.

Per serving: 400 calories, 15g protein, 20g fats, 40g carbs

Quinoa and Roasted Veggie Tacos

INGREDIENTS

Prep. time: 10 min   Cook time: 20 min   Serves: 2

- 1/2 cup quinoa, rinsed
- 1 cup vegetable broth or water
- 1 cup mixed vegetables (e.g., bell peppers, zucchini, red onion), chopped
- 1 tbsp olive oil
- 1 tsp cumin
- 1 tsp chili powder
- Salt and pepper to taste
- 4 small corn tortillas
- 1/4 cup chopped fresh cilantro (optional)
- 1/2 avocado, sliced (optional)
- Lime wedges for serving (optional)

DIRECTIONS

Cook quinoa: In a pot, combine quinoa and vegetable broth. Bring to a boil, reduce heat, cover, and simmer for 15 minutes until quinoa is cooked and liquid is absorbed.

Roast vegetables: Preheat oven to 400°F (200°C). Toss mixed vegetables with olive oil, cumin, chili powder, salt, and pepper. Spread on a baking sheet and roast for 15-20 minutes until tender.

Warm tortillas: Heat tortillas in a dry pan over medium heat for about 30 seconds on each side until warm and pliable.

Assemble tacos: Divide cooked quinoa and roasted vegetables among the tortillas.

Serve: Top with fresh cilantro, avocado slices, and lime wedges if desired.

Optional toppings: Add a drizzle of hot sauce or a dollop of vegan sour cream for extra flavor.

Per serving: 350 calories, 10g protein, 12g fats, 50g carbs

Black Bean and Avocado Tacos

INGREDIENTS

Prep. time: 10 min   Cook time: 10 min   Serves: 2

- 1/2 can (7.5 oz) black beans, rinsed and drained
- 1/2 avocado, diced
- 1/4 cup corn kernels (fresh or frozen)
- 1/4 cup diced red onion
- 1/4 cup diced tomatoes
- 2 tbsp chopped fresh cilantro
- 1/2 tbsp lime juice
- 1/2 tsp ground cumin
- 1/4 tsp chili powder
- Salt and pepper to taste
- 4 small corn tortillas

DIRECTIONS

Cook beans: In a pan, heat black beans over medium heat with cumin, chili powder, salt, and pepper for about 5 minutes until heated through.

Prepare topping: In a bowl, combine diced avocado, corn, red onion, tomatoes, cilantro, and lime juice.

Warm tortillas: Heat tortillas in a dry pan over medium heat for about 30 seconds on each side until warm and pliable.

Assemble tacos: Divide the black beans among the tortillas, top with the avocado mixture.

Serve: Enjoy immediately.

Optional toppings: Add a dollop of vegan sour cream, hot sauce, or shredded lettuce for extra flavor and texture.

Per serving: 220 calories, 8g protein, 8g fats, 30g carbs

Chickpea Shawarma Wraps

INGREDIENTS

Prep. time: 10 min   Cook time: 10 min   Serves: 2

- 1 can (15 oz) chickpeas, rinsed and drained
- 1 tsp ground cumin
- 1 tsp ground paprika
- 1 tbsp olive oil
- 1/2 cup sliced cucumber
- 1/2 cup diced tomatoes
- 2 large tortillas or flatbreads
- 1/4 cup vegan yogurt or tahini sauce
- Salt to taste

DIRECTIONS

Prepare chickpeas: In a bowl, combine chickpeas, cumin, paprika, olive oil, and salt. Mix well.

Cook chickpeas: Heat a pan over medium heat. Add the seasoned chickpeas and cook for about 5-7 minutes, stirring occasionally until chickpeas are slightly crispy.

Prepare vegetables: In a bowl, mix cucumber and tomatoes.

Warm tortillas: Heat tortillas in a dry pan over medium heat for about 30 seconds on each side until warm and pliable.

Assemble wraps: Spread a layer of vegan yogurt or tahini sauce on each tortilla. Add a portion of the cooked chickpeas and top with the cucumber and tomato mixture.

Serve: Wrap up the tortillas and enjoy immediately.

Optional toppings: Add a sprinkle of fresh parsley, a drizzle of lemon juice, or a pinch of red pepper flakes for extra flavor.

Per serving: 350 calories, 10g protein, 14g fats, 45g carbs

Quinoa and Beet Burgers

INGREDIENTS

Prep. time: 15 min   Cook time: 20 min   Serves: 2

- 1/2 cup cooked quinoa
- 1/2 cup grated beets
- 1/4 cup breadcrumbs (use gluten-free if needed)
- 1/4 cup finely chopped onion
- 1 clove garlic, minced
- 1 tbsp ground flaxseed mixed with 2.5 tbsp water (flax egg)
- 1 tsp ground cumin
- 1/2 tsp salt
- 1/4 tsp black pepper
- 1 tbsp olive oil
- 2 burger buns (use gluten-free if needed)

DIRECTIONS

Preheat oven: Preheat to 375°F (190°C).
Prepare mixture: In a bowl, combine cooked quinoa, grated beets, breadcrumbs, onion, garlic, flax egg, cumin, salt, and pepper. Mix until well combined.
Form patties: Shape the mixture into two patties.
Cook patties: Heat olive oil in a pan over medium heat. Cook patties for 3-4 minutes on each side until browned.
Bake: Transfer patties to a baking sheet and bake for 10-15 minutes until firm.
Assemble burgers: Place patties on burger buns and add your favorite toppings.

Optional toppings: Add avocado slices, lettuce, tomato, vegan mayo, or pickles for extra flavor.

Per serving: 320 calories, 9g protein, 10g fats, 48g carbs

Black Bean and Sweet Potato Burgers

INGREDIENTS

Prep. time: 15 min   Cook time: 20 min   Serves: 2

DIRECTIONS

- 1 cup black beans, rinsed and drained
- 1 cup sweet potato, cooked and mashed
- 1/2 cup breadcrumbs (use gluten-free if needed)
- 1/4 cup red onion, finely chopped
- 1 clove garlic, minced
- 1 tsp ground cumin
- 1/2 tsp chili powder
- 1/2 tsp salt
- 1/4 tsp black pepper
- 1 tbsp olive oil
- 2 burger buns (use gluten-free if needed)

Preheat oven: Preheat to 375°F (190°C).
Prepare mixture: In a bowl, mash black beans with a fork. Add sweet potato, breadcrumbs, red onion, garlic, cumin, chili powder, salt, and pepper. Mix until well combined.
Form patties: Shape the mixture into two patties.
Cook patties: Heat olive oil in a pan over medium heat. Cook patties for 3-4 minutes on each side until browned.
Bake: Transfer patties to a baking sheet and bake for 10-15 minutes until firm.
Assemble burgers: Place patties on burger buns and add your favorite toppings.

Optional toppings: Add avocado slices, lettuce, tomato, vegan mayo, or pickles for extra flavor.

Per serving: 350 calories, 10g protein, 10g fats, 55g carbs

Chickpea Salad Sandwiches

INGREDIENTS

Prep. time: 10 min   Cook time: 0 min   Serves: 2

- 1 can (15 oz) chickpeas, rinsed and drained
- 1 tbsp Dijon mustard
- 1 tbsp lemon juice
- 1 tbsp olive oil
- 1/4 cup celery, finely chopped
- 1/4 cup red onion, finely chopped
- 1/4 cup dill pickles, finely chopped (optional)
- 1 tsp dried dill (or 1 tbsp fresh dill, chopped)
- Salt and pepper to taste
- 4 slices whole grain bread (use gluten-free if needed)
- Lettuce leaves and tomato slices (optional, for serving)

DIRECTIONS

Mash chickpeas: In a bowl, mash chickpeas with a fork until slightly chunky.
Mix ingredients: Add Dijon mustard, lemon juice, olive oil, celery, red onion, pickles (if using), dill, salt, and pepper. Mix until well combined.
Assemble sandwiches: Spread chickpea salad on two slices of bread. Top with lettuce and tomato if desired, then place remaining bread slices on top.
Serve: Cut sandwiches in half and enjoy.

Optional toppings: Add avocado slices or cucumber slices for extra crunch and flavor.

Per serving: 320 calories, 10g protein, 12g fats, 42g carbs

Grilled Veggie and Pesto Paninis

INGREDIENTS

Prep. time: 10 min   Cook time: 10 min   Serves: 2

DIRECTIONS

- 1 zucchini, sliced
- 1 red bell pepper, sliced
- 1/2 red onion, sliced
- 1 tbsp olive oil
- Salt and pepper to taste
- 4 slices whole grain bread (use gluten-free if needed)
- 1/4 cup pesto (store-bought or homemade vegan pesto)
- 1/2 cup spinach leaves
- 1/4 cup vegan cheese (optional)

Preheat grill: Preheat grill or grill pan over medium-high heat.
Grill veggies: Toss zucchini, bell pepper, and red onion with olive oil, salt, and pepper. Grill vegetables for about 3-5 minutes on each side until tender and slightly charred.
Assemble paninis: Spread pesto on one side of each slice of bread. Layer grilled vegetables, spinach leaves, and vegan cheese (if using) on two slices of bread. Top with the remaining bread slices, pesto side down.
Grill paninis: Place the assembled sandwiches on the grill or in a panini press. Grill for about 3-4 minutes on each side until the bread is golden brown and crispy, and the cheese (if using) is melted.
Serve: Slice paninis in half and serve immediately.

Optional toppings: Add avocado slices, tomato slices, or a drizzle of balsamic glaze for extra flavor.

Per serving: 350 calories, 10g protein, 14g fats, 45g carbs

Classic Veggie Burger with Avocado

INGREDIENTS

Prep. time: 15 min   Cook time: 10 min   Serves: 2

- 1 cup black beans, rinsed and drained
- 1/2 cup breadcrumbs (use gluten-free if needed)
- 1/4 cup grated carrot
- 1/4 cup finely chopped onion
- 1 clove garlic, minced
- 1 tbsp ground flaxseed mixed with 2.5 tbsp water (flax egg)
- 1 tsp ground cumin
- 1/2 tsp smoked paprika
- Salt and pepper to taste
- 1 tbsp olive oil
- 2 burger buns (gluten-free)
- 1 avocado, sliced
- Lettuce leaves and tomato slices

DIRECTIONS

Prepare mixture: In a bowl, mash black beans with a fork until slightly chunky. Add breadcrumbs, grated carrot, onion, garlic, flax egg, cumin, smoked paprika, salt, and pepper. Mix until well combined.
Form patties: Shape the mixture into two patties.
Cook patties: Heat olive oil in a pan over medium heat. Cook patties for 4-5 minutes on each side until browned and heated through.
Assemble burgers: Place patties on burger buns. Top with avocado slices, lettuce, and tomato if desired.
Serve: Enjoy immediately.

Optional toppings: Add a drizzle of vegan mayo, ketchup, or mustard for extra flavor.

Per serving: 350 calories, 12g protein, 14g fats, 45g carbs

Mediterranean Veggie Sandwich

INGREDIENTS

Prep. time: 10 min   Cook time: 0 min   Serves: 2

- 4 slices whole grain bread (use gluten-free if needed)
- 1/2 cup hummus
- 1/2 cup cucumber, thinly sliced
- 1/2 cup roasted red peppers, sliced
- 1/4 cup red onion, thinly sliced
- 1/4 cup Kalamata olives, pitted and sliced
- 1/2 cup spinach leaves
- 1 tbsp olive oil
- 1 tbsp balsamic vinegar
- Salt and pepper to taste

DIRECTIONS

Prepare spread: Spread hummus on one side of each slice of bread.
Assemble sandwich: Layer cucumber, roasted red peppers, red onion, Kalamata olives, and spinach leaves on two slices of bread. Drizzle with olive oil and balsamic vinegar, and season with salt and pepper.
Top and serve: Place the remaining bread slices on top to form sandwiches. Slice in half and serve immediately.

Optional toppings: Add crumbled vegan feta or sun-dried tomatoes for extra flavor.

Per serving: 300 calories, 8g protein, 12g fats, 40g carbs

Pizza

Classic Margherita Vegan Pizza

INGREDIENTS

Prep. time: 20 min   Cook time: 15 min   Serves: 2

Pizza Crust:

- 1 cup all-purpose flour
- 1/2 cup warm water
- 1 tsp active dry yeast
- 1/2 tsp sugar
- 1/2 tsp salt
- 1 tbsp olive oil

Toppings:

- 1/2 cup tomato sauce
- 1 cup shredded vegan mozzarella cheese
- 1 large tomato, thinly sliced
- 1 tbsp olive oil
- 1 tsp dried oregano
- Salt and pepper to taste
- Fresh basil leaves

DIRECTIONS

Prepare crust: Mix warm water, sugar, and yeast. Let sit 5 min. Combine flour and salt. Add yeast mixture and olive oil. Mix to form dough. Knead 5 min. Let rise 30 min.
Preheat oven: Preheat to 475°F (245°C).
Prepare toppings: Slice tomatoes.
Assemble pizza: Roll out dough to 12-inch circle. Place on baking sheet. Spread tomato sauce over crust. Add cheese and tomato slices. Drizzle with olive oil, sprinkle oregano, salt, and pepper.
Bake: Bake 12-15 min, until crust is golden and cheese melted.
Serve: Top with fresh basil leaves. Slice and serve hot.

Optional toppings: Add red pepper flakes or a drizzle of balsamic glaze.

Per serving: 320 calories, 10g protein, 14g fats, 42g carbs

Mushroom and Spinach White Pizza

INGREDIENTS

Prep. time: 20 min   Cook time: 15 min   Serves: 2

Pizza Crust:

- 1 cup all-purpose flour
- 1/2 cup warm water
- 1 tsp active dry yeast
- 1/2 tsp sugar
- 1/2 tsp salt
- 1 tbsp olive oil

Toppings:

- 1 cup mushrooms, sliced
- 1 cup fresh spinach, chopped
- 1 cup shredded vegan mozzarella cheese
- 1 tbsp olive oil
- 2 cloves garlic, minced
- 1 tsp dried oregano
- Salt and pepper to taste

DIRECTIONS

Prepare crust: Mix warm water, sugar, and yeast. Let sit 5 min. Combine flour and salt. Add yeast mixture and olive oil. Mix to form dough. Knead 5 min. Let rise 30 min.
Preheat oven: Preheat to 475°F (245°C).
Prepare toppings: Heat olive oil in a pan, cook garlic 1 min. Slice mushrooms and chop spinach.
Assemble pizza: Roll out dough to 12-inch circle. Place on baking sheet. Brush with garlic oil. Add cheese, mushrooms, spinach, oregano, salt, and pepper.
Bake: Bake 12-15 min, until crust is golden and cheese melted.
Serve: Slice and serve hot.

Optional toppings: Add red pepper flakes, truffle oil, or vegan Parmesan.

Per serving: 320 calories, 10g protein, 14g fats, 42g carbs

Pizza

Pineapple and Tempeh Hawaiian Pizza

INGREDIENTS

Prep. time: 20 min   Cook time: 15 min   Serves: 2

Pizza Crust:

- 1 cup all-purpose flour (use gluten-free if needed)
- 1/2 cup warm water
- 1 tsp active dry yeast
- 1/2 tsp sugar
- 1/2 tsp salt
- 1 tbsp olive oil

Toppings:

- 1/2 cup tomato sauce
- 1 cup shredded vegan mozzarella cheese
- 1/2 cup pineapple chunks
- 1/2 cup tempeh, cubed
- Salt and pepper to taste

DIRECTIONS

Prepare crust: Mix warm water, sugar, and yeast. Let sit 5 min. Combine flour and salt. Add yeast mixture and olive oil. Mix to form dough. Knead 5 min. Let rise 30 min.
Preheat oven: Preheat to 475°F (245°C).
Prepare toppings: Lightly sauté tempeh cubes until golden.
Assemble pizza: Roll out dough to 12-inch circle. Place on baking sheet. Spread tomato sauce over crust. Add cheese, pineapple chunks, and tempeh. Sprinkle with salt and pepper.
Bake: Bake 12-15 min, until crust is golden and cheese melted.
Serve: Slice and serve hot.

Optional toppings: Add fresh basil leaves, red pepper flakes, or a drizzle of vegan ranch dressing.

Per serving: 320 calories, 12g protein, 14g fats, 42g carbs

Caramelized Onion and Arugula Pizza

INGREDIENTS

Prep. time: 20 min   Cook time: 15 min   Serves: 2

DIRECTIONS

Pizza Crust:

- 1 cup all-purpose flour (use gluten-free if needed)
- 1/2 cup warm water
- 1 tsp active dry yeast
- 1/2 tsp sugar
- 1/2 tsp salt
- 1 tbsp olive oil

Toppings:

- 2 large onions, thinly sliced
- 1 tbsp olive oil (for caramelizing onions)
- 1 cup shredded vegan mozzarella cheese
- 1 cup fresh arugula
- Salt and pepper to taste

Prepare crust: Mix warm water, sugar, and yeast. Let sit 5 min. Combine flour and salt. Add yeast mixture and olive oil. Mix to form dough. Knead 5 min. Let rise 30 min.
Preheat oven: Preheat to 475°F (245°C).
Caramelize onions: In a pan, heat olive oil over medium heat. Add sliced onions and cook, stirring occasionally, until onions are caramelized, about 15 minutes.
Assemble pizza: Roll out dough to 12-inch circle. Place on baking sheet. Sprinkle vegan mozzarella cheese evenly over the crust. Add caramelized onions.
Bake: Bake 12-15 min, until crust is golden and cheese melted.
Add arugula: Remove pizza from oven and top with fresh arugula. Season with salt and pepper.
Serve: Slice and serve hot.

Optional toppings: Add a drizzle of balsamic glaze or a sprinkle of red pepper flakes for extra flavor.

Per serving: 300 calories, 10g protein, 14g fats, 40g carbs

Chapter 11: Said Dishes
Vegetable Sides

Rosemary Sweet Potato Wedges

INGREDIENTS

- 4 large sweet potatoes, cut into wedges
- 4 tbsp olive oil
- 2 tbsp fresh rosemary, chopped (or 2 tsp dried rosemary)
- 1 tsp garlic powder
- 1 tsp salt
- 1/2 tsp black pepper

Prep. time: 10 min   Cook time: 25 min   Serves: 4

DIRECTIONS

Preheat oven: Preheat to 425°F (220°C).
Prepare potatoes: In a large bowl, toss sweet potato wedges with olive oil, rosemary, garlic powder, salt, and pepper until evenly coated.
Bake: Arrange wedges in a single layer on a baking sheet. Bake for 20-25 minutes, turning once halfway through, until golden brown and crispy.
Serve: Remove from oven and let cool slightly before serving.

Optional toppings: Add a sprinkle of sea salt or a drizzle of balsamic glaze for extra flavor.

Per serving: 220 calories, 4g protein, 10g fats, 30g carbs

Garlic Roasted Brussels Sprouts

INGREDIENTS

- 1.5 lbs Brussels sprouts, trimmed and halved
- 3 tbsp olive oil
- 4 cloves garlic, minced
- 1 tsp salt
- 1/2 tsp black pepper

Prep. time: 10 min   Cook time: 25 min   Serves: 4

DIRECTIONS

Preheat oven: Preheat to 400°F (200°C).
Prepare Brussels sprouts: In a large bowl, toss Brussels sprouts with olive oil, minced garlic, salt, and pepper until evenly coated.
Bake: Arrange Brussels sprouts in a single layer on a baking sheet. Bake for 20-25 minutes, shaking the pan halfway through, until they are golden brown and crispy.
Serve: Remove from oven and let cool slightly before serving.

Optional toppings: Add a sprinkle of lemon zest, a drizzle of balsamic glaze, or a handful of toasted pine nuts for extra flavor.

Per serving: 150 calories, 4g protein, 10g fats, 12g carbs

Maple Roasted Butternut Squash

INGREDIENTS

Prep. time: 10 min   Cook time: 30 min   Serves: 4

- 1 large butternut squash, peeled, seeded, and cubed
- 3 tbsp olive oil
- 2 tbsp maple syrup
- 1 tsp ground cinnamon
- 1/2 tsp salt
- 1/4 tsp black pepper

DIRECTIONS

Preheat oven: Preheat to 400°F (200°C).
Prepare squash: In a large bowl, toss butternut squash cubes with olive oil, maple syrup, cinnamon, salt, and pepper until evenly coated.
Bake: Arrange squash in a single layer on a baking sheet. Bake for 25-30 minutes, stirring halfway through, until tender and caramelized.
Serve: Remove from oven and let cool slightly before serving.

Optional toppings: Add a sprinkle of chopped pecans or a drizzle of balsamic glaze for extra flavor.

Per serving: 200 calories, 2g protein, 11g fats, 26g carbs

Balsamic Glazed Carrots

INGREDIENTS

Prep. time: 10 min   Cook time: 25 min   Serves: 4

DIRECTIONS

- 1 lb carrots, peeled and cut into sticks
- 2 tbsp olive oil
- 1/4 cup balsamic vinegar
- 2 tbsp maple syrup
- 1 tsp dried thyme
- 1/2 tsp salt
- 1/4 tsp black pepper

Preheat oven: Preheat to 400°F (200°C).
Prepare carrots: In a large bowl, toss carrot sticks with olive oil, balsamic vinegar, maple syrup, thyme, salt, and pepper until evenly coated.
Bake: Arrange carrots in a single layer on a baking sheet. Bake for 20-25 minutes, stirring halfway through, until tender and caramelized.
Serve: Remove from oven and let cool slightly before serving.

Optional toppings: Add a sprinkle of chopped fresh parsley or a drizzle of additional balsamic glaze for extra flavor.

Per serving: 120 calories, 1g protein, 7g fats, 15g carbs

Vegetable Sides

Crispy Parmesan Cauliflower

INGREDIENTS

Prep. time: 10 min   Cook time: 25 min   Serves: 4

- 1 large head of cauliflower, cut into florets
- 3 tbsp olive oil
- 1/2 cup vegan Parmesan cheese
- 1/2 cup breadcrumbs (use gluten-free if needed)
- 1 tsp garlic powder
- 1 tsp dried oregano
- 1/2 tsp salt
- 1/4 tsp black pepper

DIRECTIONS

Preheat oven: Preheat to 425°F (220°C).
Prepare coating: In a large bowl, combine vegan Parmesan, breadcrumbs, garlic powder, oregano, salt, and pepper.
Coat cauliflower: Toss cauliflower florets with olive oil in a separate bowl. Then, coat each floret in the breadcrumb mixture, pressing gently to adhere.
Bake: Arrange coated cauliflower in a single layer on a baking sheet. Bake for 20-25 minutes, turning once halfway through, until golden and crispy.
Serve: Remove from oven and let cool slightly before serving.

Optional toppings: Add a sprinkle of fresh parsley or a squeeze of lemon juice for extra flavor.

Per serving: 180 calories, 5g protein, 10g fats, 15g carbs

Roasted Garlic Mushrooms

INGREDIENTS

Prep. time: 10 min   Cook time: 20 min   Serves: 4

DIRECTIONS

- 1 lb mushrooms, cleaned and halved
- 3 tbsp olive oil
- 4 cloves garlic, minced
- 1 tsp dried thyme
- 1/2 tsp salt
- 1/4 tsp black pepper
- 1 tbsp balsamic vinegar (optional)
- 2 tbsp fresh parsley, chopped (optional)

Preheat oven: Preheat to 400°F (200°C).
Prepare mushrooms: In a large bowl, toss mushrooms with olive oil, minced garlic, thyme, salt, and pepper until evenly coated.
Bake: Arrange mushrooms in a single layer on a baking sheet. Roast for 15-20 minutes, stirring halfway through, until tender and golden brown.
Optional glaze: Drizzle with balsamic vinegar if desired, and toss to coat.
Serve: Garnish with fresh parsley before serving.

Optional toppings: Add a sprinkle of red pepper flakes or a drizzle of lemon juice for extra flavor.

Per serving: 120 calories, 3g protein, 10g fats, 5g carbs

Grains and Legumes

Lemon Herb Quinoa Pilaf

INGREDIENTS

Prep. time: 10 min   Cook time: 20 min   Serves: 4

- 1 cup quinoa, rinsed
- 2 cups vegetable broth or water
- 1 tbsp olive oil
- 1 small onion, finely chopped
- 2 cloves garlic, minced
- 1 lemon, zested and juiced
- 1/4 cup fresh parsley, chopped
- 1/4 cup fresh cilantro, chopped
- 1 tsp dried oregano
- Salt and pepper to taste

DIRECTIONS

Cook quinoa: In a medium saucepan, bring vegetable broth to a boil. Add rinsed quinoa, reduce heat to low, cover, and simmer for 15 minutes or until quinoa is tender and liquid is absorbed.
Prepare aromatics: In a large bowl, combine chopped onion, minced garlic, lemon zest, lemon juice, parsley, cilantro, oregano, salt, and pepper.
Combine ingredients: Fluff the cooked quinoa with a fork and add it to the bowl with the prepared aromatics.
Mix and serve: Stir well to combine all the flavors and serve hot.

Optional toppings: Add toasted pine nuts or a sprinkle of vegan Parmesan for extra flavor.

Per serving: 180 calories, 5g protein, 6g fats, 28g carbs

Coconut Curry Chickpeas

INGREDIENTS

Prep. time: 10 min   Cook time: 20 min   Serves: 4

- 1 tbsp olive oil
- 1 small onion, finely chopped
- 2 cloves garlic, minced
- 1 tbsp ginger, minced
- 1 tbsp curry powder
- 1 can (15 oz) chickpeas, rinsed and drained
- 1 can (14 oz) coconut milk
- 1 cup diced tomatoes (fresh or canned)
- 1 tbsp tomato paste
- 1 tsp ground cumin
- 1 tsp ground coriander
- Salt and pepper to taste
- 1/4 cup fresh cilantro, chopped (optional, for garnish)

DIRECTIONS

Heat oil: In a large pan, heat olive oil over medium heat. Add chopped onion and cook until softened, about 5 minutes.
Add aromatics: Stir in garlic and ginger; cook for another 1-2 minutes until fragrant.
Add spices: Mix in curry powder, ground cumin, and ground coriander, stirring for 1 minute.
Combine ingredients: Add chickpeas, coconut milk, diced tomatoes, and tomato paste. Stir well to combine.
Simmer: Bring to a simmer and cook for 15-20 minutes, stirring occasionally, until the sauce thickens and flavors meld.
Season: Add salt and pepper to taste.
Serve: Garnish with chopped fresh cilantro if desired. Serve hot over rice or with naan bread.

Optional toppings: Add a squeeze of lime juice or a sprinkle of red pepper flakes for extra flavor.

Per serving: 300 calories, 10g protein, 18g fats, 25g carbs

Grains and Legumes

Turmeric and Ginger Millet

INGREDIENTS

Prep. time: 10 min   Cook time: 25 min   Serves: 4

- 1 cup millet, rinsed
- 2 cups vegetable broth or water
- 1 tbsp olive oil
- 1 small onion, finely chopped
- 2 cloves garlic, minced
- 1 tbsp ginger, minced
- 1 tsp ground turmeric
- 1/2 tsp ground cumin
- 1/2 tsp ground coriander
- Salt and pepper to taste
- 1/4 cup fresh parsley, chopped (optional, for garnish)

DIRECTIONS

Cook millet: In a medium saucepan, bring vegetable broth to a boil. Add rinsed millet, reduce heat to low, cover, and simmer for 15-20 minutes until millet is tender and liquid is absorbed.
Prepare aromatics: In a large pan, heat olive oil over medium heat. Add chopped onion and cook until softened, about 5 minutes. Stir in garlic and ginger; cook for another 1-2 minutes.
Add spices: Mix in ground turmeric, cumin, and coriander, stirring for 1 minute until fragrant.
Combine ingredients: Add cooked millet to the pan with the aromatics and spices. Stir well to combine.
Season: Add salt and pepper to taste.
Serve: Garnish with chopped fresh parsley if desired. Serve hot.

Optional toppings: Add a squeeze of lemon juice or a handful of toasted nuts for extra flavor.

Per serving: 220 calories, 6g protein, 8g fats, 32g carbs

Spiced Lentil and Rice Pilaf

INGREDIENTS

Prep. time: 10 min   Cook time: 30 min   Serves: 4

- 1 cup basmati rice, rinsed
- 1/2 cup dried green or brown lentils, rinsed
- 3 cups vegetable broth or water
- 1 tbsp olive oil
- 1 small onion, finely chopped
- 2 cloves garlic, minced
- 1 tbsp ginger, minced
- 1 tsp ground cumin
- 1 tsp ground coriander
- 1/2 tsp ground turmeric
- 1/2 tsp ground cinnamon
- Salt and pepper to taste
- 1/4 cup fresh cilantro or parsley, chopped (optional, for garnish)

DIRECTIONS

Cook lentils: In a medium saucepan, bring 2 cups of vegetable broth to a boil. Add lentils, reduce heat, cover, and simmer for 15 minutes until lentils are tender but not mushy. Drain any excess liquid.
Prepare aromatics: Heat oil, cook onion 5 min, add garlic and ginger 1-2 min.
Add spices: Mix in ground cumin, coriander, turmeric, and cinnamon, stirring for 1 minute until fragrant.
Combine and cook: Add rice, lentils, and 1 cup broth. Boil, reduce heat, cover, and simmer 15-20 min until rice is tender.
Season and serve: Add salt, pepper, and garnish with cilantro or parsley.

Optional toppings: Add toasted almonds or raisins.

Per serving: 280 calories, 10g protein, 6g fats, 50g carbs

Creamy Coconut Lentil Dal

INGREDIENTS

Prep. time: 10 min   Cook time: 30 min   Serves: 4

- 1 cup red lentils, rinsed
- 1 can (14 oz) coconut milk
- 2 cups vegetable broth or water
- 1 tbsp olive oil
- 1 small onion, finely chopped
- 2 cloves garlic, minced
- 1 tbsp ginger, minced
- 1 tbsp curry powder
- 1 tsp ground cumin
- 1 tsp ground turmeric
- 1/2 tsp ground coriander
- 1/2 tsp salt
- 1/4 tsp black pepper
- 1/4 cup fresh cilantro, chopped (optional, for garnish)

DIRECTIONS

Prepare aromatics: Heat olive oil in a large pot over medium heat. Cook onion for 5 minutes until softened. Add garlic and ginger, cook for 1 minute.

Add spices: Stir in curry powder, cumin, turmeric, and coriander, cooking for 1 minute until fragrant.

Cook lentils: Add lentils, coconut milk, and vegetable broth. Bring to a boil, reduce heat, and simmer for 20-25 minutes until lentils are tender.

Season and serve: Add salt and pepper to taste. Garnish with fresh cilantro if desired. Serve hot.

Optional toppings: Add a squeeze of lime juice or a drizzle of chili oil for extra flavor.

Per serving: 320 calories, 10g protein, 18g fats, 28g carbs

Wild Rice and Mushroom Pilaf

INGREDIENTS

Prep. time: 10 min   Cook time: 40 min   Serves: 4

- 1 cup wild rice, rinsed
- 2 cups vegetable broth or water
- 1 tbsp olive oil
- 1 small onion, finely chopped
- 2 cloves garlic, minced
- 2 cups mushrooms, sliced
- 1 tsp dried thyme
- 1/2 tsp salt
- 1/4 tsp black pepper
- 1/4 cup fresh parsley, chopped (optional, for garnish)

DIRECTIONS

Cook rice: In a medium saucepan, bring vegetable broth to a boil. Add wild rice, reduce heat, cover, and simmer for 35-40 minutes until rice is tender and liquid is absorbed.

Prepare aromatics: In a large pan, heat olive oil over medium heat. Cook onion for 5 minutes until softened. Add garlic and cook for 1 minute.

Add mushrooms and spices: Add sliced mushrooms, thyme, salt, and pepper. Cook for 8-10 minutes until mushrooms are tender and browned.

Combine and serve: Add cooked wild rice to the mushroom mixture and stir to combine. Garnish with fresh parsley if desired. Serve hot.

Optional toppings: Add toasted nuts or a drizzle of truffle oil for extra flavor.

Per serving: 200 calories, 6g protein, 7g fats, 32g carbs

Chapter 12: Desserts
Cookies and Bars

Double Chocolate Brownie Bites

INGREDIENTS

- 1/2 cup almond flour
- 2 tbsp cocoa powder
- 1/4 cup coconut sugar
- 2 tbsp melted coconut oil
- 2 tbsp almond milk
- 1/2 tsp vanilla extract
- 1/4 tsp baking powder
- 1/8 tsp salt
- 1/4 cup dairy-free chocolate chips

Prep. time: 10 min   Cook time: 15 min   Serves: 2

DIRECTIONS

Preheat oven: Preheat to 350°F (175°C).
Prepare batter: In a bowl, mix almond flour, cocoa powder, coconut sugar, baking powder, and salt. Add melted coconut oil, almond milk, and vanilla extract. Stir until well combined. Fold in chocolate chips.
Portion batter: Scoop batter into a greased mini muffin tin, filling each cup about 3/4 full.
Bake: Bake for 12-15 minutes, or until a toothpick inserted into the center comes out clean.
Cool and serve: Let brownie bites cool in the tin for 10 minutes before transferring to a wire rack to cool completely.

Optional toppings: Dust with powdered sugar or drizzle with melted chocolate for extra indulgence.

Per serving: 220 calories, 5g protein, 15g fats, 20g carbs

Almond Butter Oatmeal Bars

INGREDIENTS

- 1/2 cup rolled oats
- 1/4 cup almond butter
- 2 tbsp maple syrup
- 1/4 cup almond flour
- 1/4 tsp vanilla extract
- 1/8 tsp salt
- 1/4 tsp cinnamon (optional)
- 1/4 cup dairy-free chocolate chips (optional)

Prep. time: 10 min   Cook time: 15 min   Serves: 2

DIRECTIONS

Preheat oven: Preheat to 350°F (175°C).
Prepare mixture: In a bowl, mix rolled oats, almond flour, and salt (and cinnamon if using). In a separate bowl, combine almond butter, maple syrup, and vanilla extract until smooth. Pour the wet mixture into the dry mixture and stir until well combined. Fold in chocolate chips if using.
Press into pan: Press the mixture into a greased or parchment-lined small baking pan, about 8x4 inches.
Bake: Bake for 12-15 minutes until edges are golden and the center is set.
Cool and cut: Let cool completely in the pan before cutting into bars.

Optional toppings: Drizzle with melted chocolate or sprinkle with shredded coconut for extra flavor.

Per serving: 250 calories, 7g protein, 16g fats, 20g carbs

Cookies and Bars

Cranberry Pistachio Cookies

INGREDIENTS

Prep. time: 10 min   Cook time: 12 min   Serves: 2

- 1/4 cup almond flour
- 1/4 cup rolled oats
- 2 tbsp coconut oil, melted
- 2 tbsp maple syrup
- 1/4 tsp vanilla extract
- 1/8 tsp baking soda
- 1/8 tsp salt
- 2 tbsp dried cranberries
- 2 tbsp shelled pistachios, chopped

DIRECTIONS

Preheat oven: Preheat to 350°F (175°C).
Prepare dough: In a bowl, mix almond flour, rolled oats, baking soda, and salt. In a separate bowl, combine melted coconut oil, maple syrup, and vanilla extract. Pour the wet mixture into the dry mixture and stir until well combined. Fold in dried cranberries and chopped pistachios.
Form cookies: Scoop tablespoons of dough onto a baking sheet lined with parchment paper, flattening each slightly with the back of a spoon.
Bake: Bake for 10-12 minutes until edges are golden.
Cool and serve: Let cookies cool on the baking sheet for 5 minutes before transferring to a wire rack to cool completely.

Optional toppings: Drizzle with melted white chocolate or sprinkle with additional chopped pistachios for extra flavor.

Per serving: 220 calories, 5g protein, 14g fats, 18g carbs

Spiced Ginger Molasses Cookies

INGREDIENTS

Prep. time: 10 min   Cook time: 12 min   Serves: 2

- 1/4 cup almond flour
- 1/4 cup whole wheat flour (or gluten-free flour)
- 2 tbsp coconut oil, melted
- 2 tbsp maple syrup
- 1 tbsp coconut sugar
- 1/4 tsp vanilla extract
- 1/4 tsp baking soda
- 1/8 tsp salt
- 1/2 tsp ground ginger
- 1/4 tsp ground cinnamon
- 1/8 tsp ground cloves

DIRECTIONS

Preheat oven: Preheat to 350°F (175°C).
Prepare dough: In a bowl, mix almond flour, whole wheat flour, baking soda, salt, ground ginger, cinnamon, and cloves. In a separate bowl, combine melted coconut oil, maple syrup, coconut sugar, and vanilla extract. Pour the wet mixture into the dry mixture and stir until well combined.
Form cookies: Scoop tablespoons of dough onto a baking sheet lined with parchment paper, flattening each slightly with the back of a spoon.
Bake: Bake for 10-12 minutes until edges are golden.
Cool and serve: Let cookies cool on the baking sheet for 5 minutes before transferring to a wire rack to cool completely.

Optional toppings: Roll the dough balls in coconut sugar before baking for a sweet, crunchy exterior.

Per serving: 220 calories, 4g protein, 12g fats, 27g carbs

Lemon Coconut Bliss Bars

INGREDIENTS

Prep. time: 10 min   Cook time: 15 min   Serves: 2

- 1/2 cup almond flour
- 1/4 cup shredded coconut (unsweetened)
- 2 tbsp coconut oil, melted
- 2 tbsp maple syrup
- 1 tbsp lemon juice
- 1 tsp lemon zest
- 1/4 tsp vanilla extract
- 1/8 tsp salt

DIRECTIONS

Preheat oven: Preheat to 350°F (175°C).
Prepare mixture: In a bowl, mix almond flour, shredded coconut, and salt. In a separate bowl, combine melted coconut oil, maple syrup, lemon juice, lemon zest, and vanilla extract. Pour the wet mixture into the dry mixture and stir until well combined.
Press into pan: Press the mixture into a greased or parchment-lined small baking pan, about 8x4 inches.
Bake: Bake for 12-15 minutes until the edges are golden.
Cool and serve: Let the bars cool completely in the pan before cutting into squares and serving.

Optional toppings: Dust with powdered sugar or drizzle with a simple lemon glaze for extra flavor.

Per serving: 210 calories, 4g protein, 14g fats, 16g carbs

No-Bake Chocolate Peanut Butter Bars

INGREDIENTS

Prep. time: 10 min   Cook time: 0 min   Serves: 2

- 1/2 cup rolled oats
- 1/4 cup peanut butter
- 2 tbsp maple syrup
- 1/4 cup coconut oil, melted
- 1/4 cup dairy-free chocolate chips
- 1/4 tsp vanilla extract
- 1/8 tsp salt

DIRECTIONS

Prepare base: In a bowl, mix rolled oats, peanut butter, maple syrup, melted coconut oil, vanilla extract, and salt until well combined. Press the mixture into a small, greased, or parchment-lined baking pan, about 8x4 inches.
Melt chocolate: In a microwave-safe bowl, melt the dairy-free chocolate chips in 30-second intervals, stirring until smooth.
Add chocolate layer: Pour the melted chocolate over the pressed oat mixture, spreading it evenly.
Chill: Place the pan in the refrigerator for at least 1 hour until the bars are firm.
Serve: Once firm, cut into squares and serve.

Optional toppings: Sprinkle with sea salt or chopped nuts before the chocolate sets for extra flavor.

Per serving: 250 calories, 5g protein, 16g fats, 20g carbs

Cakes and Cupcakes

Rich Vegan Red Velvet Cake

INGREDIENTS

Prep. time: 15 min   Cook time: 25 min   Serves: 4

- 2 cups all-purpose flour
- 1 cup coconut sugar
- 2 tbsp cocoa powder
- 2 tsp baking powder
- 1 tsp baking soda
- 1 tsp salt
- 1 cup almond milk
- 1/2 cup vegetable oil
- 2 tbsp apple cider vinegar
- 2 tsp vanilla extract
- 2 tbsp red beet juice (for color)

For the Frosting:

- 1 cup vegan cream cheese
- 1/2 cup powdered sugar
- 1 tsp vanilla extract

DIRECTIONS

Preheat oven: Preheat to 350°F (175°C). Grease and flour an 8-inch round cake pan.

Prepare batter: Mix dry ingredients in a bowl. Combine wet ingredients in another bowl. Mix wet and dry ingredients until just combined.

Bake: Pour batter into the pan. Bake for 20-25 minutes.

Cool: Let cool in the pan for 10 minutes, then transfer to a wire rack to cool completely.

Prepare frosting: Beat together vegan cream cheese, powdered sugar, and vanilla extract until smooth.

Frost cake: Spread frosting over the cooled cake.

Serve: Slice and serve.

Optional toppings: Garnish with fresh berries or a sprinkle of cocoa powder.

Per serving: 300 calories, 5g protein, 15g fats, 35g carbs

Coconut Lime Cupcakes

INGREDIENTS

Prep. time: 15 min   Cook time: 20 min   Serves: 4

- 1 cup all-purpose flour
- 1/2 cup coconut sugar
- 1/2 tsp baking soda
- 1/4 tsp salt
- 1/2 cup coconut milk
- 1/4 cup vegetable oil
- 2 tbsp lime juice
- 1 tsp lime zest
-

For the Frosting:

- 1/2 cup vegan butter, softened
- 1 cup powdered sugar
- 1 tbsp lime juice

DIRECTIONS

Preheat oven: Preheat to 350°F (175°C). Line a muffin tin with cupcake liners.

Prepare batter: Mix dry ingredients (flour, coconut sugar, baking soda, salt) in a bowl. Combine wet ingredients (coconut milk, vegetable oil, lime juice, lime zest) in another bowl. Mix wet and dry ingredients until just combined.

Bake: Fill cupcake liners 3/4 full with batter. Bake for 18-20 minutes, until a toothpick inserted into the center comes out clean.

Cool: Let cupcakes cool in the tin for 5 minutes, then transfer to a wire rack to cool completely.

Prepare frosting: Beat together vegan butter, powdered sugar, and lime juice until smooth.

Frost cupcakes: Spread frosting over cooled cupcakes.

Serve: Top with additional lime zest if desired.

Optional toppings: Add a sprinkle of coconut flakes or a drizzle of lime glaze.

Cakes and Cupcakes

Carrot Cake with Cream Cheese Frosting

INGREDIENTS

Prep. time: 15 min   Cook time: 25 min   Serves: 4

- 1 cup all-purpose flour
- 1/2 cup coconut sugar
- 1 tsp baking powder
- 1/2 tsp baking soda
- 1/2 tsp ground cinnamon
- 1/4 tsp ground nutmeg
- 1/4 tsp salt
- 1 cup grated carrots
- 1/2 cup almond milk
- 1/4 cup vegetable oil
- 1 tsp apple cider vinegar
- 1 tsp vanilla extract

For the Frosting:

- 1/2 cup vegan cream cheese
- 1/4 cup powdered sugar
- 1 tsp vanilla extract

DIRECTIONS

Preheat oven: Preheat to 350°F (175°C). Grease and flour a 6-inch round cake pan.
Prepare batter: Mix dry ingredients in a bowl. In another bowl, combine wet ingredients. Mix wet and dry ingredients until just combined.
Bake: Pour batter into the pan. Bake for 20-25 minutes.
Cool: Let cool in the pan for 10 minutes, then transfer to a wire rack.
Prepare frosting: Beat together vegan cream cheese, powdered sugar, and vanilla extract until smooth.
Frost cake: Spread frosting over the cooled cake.
Serve: Slice and serve.

Optional toppings: Garnish with chopped walnuts or shredded coconut.

Per serving: 290 calories, 4g protein, 14g fats, 34g carbs

Strawberry Shortcake Cupcakes

INGREDIENTS

Prep. time: 15 min   Cook time: 20 min   Serves: 4

- 1 cup all-purpose flour
- 1/2 cup coconut sugar
- 1 tsp baking powder
- 1/2 tsp baking soda
- 1/4 tsp salt
- 1/2 cup almond milk
- 1/4 cup vegetable oil
- 1 tsp apple cider vinegar
- 1 tsp vanilla extract
- 1/2 cup chopped fresh strawberries

For the Frosting:

- 1/2 cup vegan whipped cream
- 1/4 cup sliced fresh strawberries

DIRECTIONS

Preheat oven: Preheat to 350°F (175°C). Line a muffin tin with cupcake liners.
Prepare batter: Mix dry ingredients in a bowl. In another bowl, combine wet. Mix wet and dry ingredients until just combined. Fold in chopped strawberries.
Bake: Fill cupcake liners 3/4 full with batter. Bake for 18-20 minutes, until a toothpick inserted into the center comes out clean.
Cool: Let cupcakes cool in the tin for 5 minutes, then transfer to a wire rack to cool completely.
Prepare frosting: Once cupcakes are cool, top with vegan whipped cream and sliced strawberries.
Serve: Enjoy immediately.

Optional toppings: Add a drizzle of strawberry sauce or a sprinkle of powdered sugar.

Per serving: 250 calories, 3g protein, 14g fats, 28g

Cakes and Cupcakes

Spiced Pumpkin Cake with Cashew Frosting

INGREDIENTS

Prep. time: 10 min   Cook time: 25 min   Serves: 4

- 1 cup all-purpose flour
- 1/2 cup coconut sugar
- 1 tsp baking powder
- 1/2 tsp baking soda
- 1/2 tsp ground cinnamon
- 1/4 tsp ground nutmeg
- 1/4 tsp salt
- 1/2 cup pumpkin puree
- 1/2 cup almond milk
- 1/4 cup vegetable oil
- 1 tsp vanilla extract

For the Frosting:

- 1/2 cup cashews, soaked
- 2 tbsp maple syrup
- 1 tbsp lemon juice

DIRECTIONS

Preheat oven: Preheat to 350°F (175°C). Grease a 6-inch round cake pan.

Prepare batter: Mix dry ingredients in a bowl. In another bowl, combine wet ingredients. Mix wet and dry ingredients until just combined.

Bake: Pour batter into the pan. Bake for 20-25 minutes.

Cool: Let cool in the pan for 10 minutes, then transfer to a wire rack.

Prepare frosting: Blend soaked cashews with maple syrup and lemon juice until smooth.

Frost cake: Spread frosting over the cooled cake.

Serve: Slice and serve.

Optional toppings: Garnish with a sprinkle of cinnamon or chopped nuts.

Per serving: 290 calories, 6g protein, 14g fats, 34g carbs

Vanilla Almond Cupcakes with Raspberry Frosting

INGREDIENTS

Prep. time: 15 min   Cook time: 20 min   Serves: 4

DIRECTIONS

- 1 cup all-purpose flour
- 1/2 cup coconut sugar
- 1 tsp baking powder
- 1/2 tsp baking soda
- 1/4 tsp salt
- 1/2 cup almond milk
- 1/4 cup vegetable oil
- 1 tsp apple cider vinegar
- 1 tsp vanilla extract
- 1/4 tsp almond extract

For the Frosting:

- 1/2 cup vegan butter, softened
- 1/2 cup powdered sugar
- 1/4 cup fresh raspberries

Preheat oven: Preheat to 350°F (175°C). Line a muffin tin with cupcake liners.

Prepare batter: Mix dry ingredients in a bowl. In another bowl, combine wet ingredients. Mix wet and dry ingredients until just combined.

Bake: Fill cupcake liners 3/4 full with batter. Bake for 18-20 minutes, until a toothpick inserted into the center comes out clean.

Cool: Let cupcakes cool in the tin for 5 minutes, then transfer to a wire rack to cool completely.

Prepare frosting: Beat together vegan butter and powdered sugar until smooth. Mash raspberries and fold them into the frosting.

Frost cupcakes: Spread frosting over cooled cupcakes.

Serve: Enjoy immediately.

Optional toppings: Garnish with fresh raspberries or a sprinkle of chopped almonds.

Per serving: 280 calories, 3g protein, 15g fats, 30g carbs

Classic Apple Pie

INGREDIENTS

Prep. time: 30 min   Cook time: 45 min   Serves: 4

For the Pie Crust:

- 1 1/2 cups all-purpose flour
- 1/2 tsp salt
- 1/2 cup vegan butter, cold and cubed
- 4-6 tbsp ice water

For the Filling:

- 4 large apples, peeled, cored, and sliced
- 1/2 cup coconut sugar
- 1 tsp ground cinnamon
- 1/4 tsp ground nutmeg
- 1 tbsp lemon juice
- 2 tbsp cornstarch
- 1 tbsp vegan butter, melted

DIRECTIONS

Prepare pie crust: Mix flour and salt, cut in cold vegan butter until it resembles coarse crumbs, then add ice water gradually until the dough comes together. Divide, shape into discs, wrap, and refrigerate for 30 minutes.
Prepare filling: Mix apple slices, coconut sugar, cinnamon, nutmeg, lemon juice, and cornstarch in a large bowl.
Assemble pie: Roll out one disc of dough for the bottom crust, fill with apple mixture, roll out the second disc for the top crust, seal edges, cut slits on top, and brush with melted vegan butter.
Bake: Preheat oven to 375°F (190°C) and bake for 45-50 minutes.
Cool and serve: Cool on a wire rack before serving.

Optional toppings: Serve with vegan vanilla ice cream or coconut whipped cream.

Per serving: 350 calories, 3g protein, 15g fats, 55g carbs

Rich Chocolate Ganache Tart

INGREDIENTS

Prep. time: 15 min   Cook time: 10 min   Serves: 4

For the Crust:

- 1 cup almond flour
- 2 tbsp cocoa powder
- 2 tbsp coconut oil, melted
- 2 tbsp maple syrup

For the Ganache:

- 1/2 cup full-fat coconut milk
- 1 cup dairy-free dark chocolate chips
- 1 tsp vanilla extract

DIRECTIONS

Instructions: Preheat oven: Preheat to 350°F (175°C). Grease a tart pan.
Prepare crust: Mix almond flour, cocoa powder, melted coconut oil, and maple syrup until well combined. Press mixture into the bottom of the tart pan.
Bake: Bake for 10 minutes. Let cool.
Prepare ganache: Heat coconut milk in a saucepan until just simmering. Remove from heat, add dark chocolate chips, and let sit for 5 minutes. Stir until smooth, then add vanilla extract.
Assemble tart: Pour ganache into the cooled crust, spreading evenly.
Chill: Chill in the refrigerator for at least 2 hours until set.
Serve: Slice and serve.

Optional toppings: Garnish with fresh berries or fruits.

Per serving: 350 calories, 6g protein, 26g fats, 22g carbs

Creamy Coconut Cream Pie

INGREDIENTS

Prep. time: 20 min   Cook time: 10 min   Serves: 4

For the Crust:

- 1 cup graham cracker crumbs
- 2 tbsp coconut oil, melted
- 2 tbsp maple syrup

For the Filling:

- 1 can (14 oz) full-fat coconut milk
- 1/2 cup coconut sugar
- 3 tbsp cornstarch
- 1/4 tsp salt
- 1 tsp vanilla extract
- 1/2 cup shredded coconut

For the Topping:

- 1/2 cup coconut whipped cream

DIRECTIONS

Prepare crust: Mix graham cracker crumbs, melted coconut oil, and maple syrup. Press into a pie pan.
Bake: Preheat oven to 350°F (175°C). Bake for 10 minutes. Let cool.
Prepare filling: Whisk coconut milk, coconut sugar, cornstarch, and salt in a saucepan. Cook over medium heat until thickened, about 5-7 minutes. Remove from heat, stir in vanilla and shredded coconut.
Assemble pie: Pour filling into the cooled crust.
Chill: Refrigerate for at least 2 hours.
Top pie: Spread coconut whipped cream over the chilled pie.
Serve: Slice and serve.

Optional toppings: Garnish with toasted coconut flakes.

Per serving: 350 calories, 4g protein, 22g fats, 34g carbs

Mixed Berry Tart with Almond Crust

INGREDIENTS

Prep. time: 15 min   Cook time: 10 min   Serves: 4

For the Crust:

- 1 cup almond flour
- 2 tbsp coconut oil, melted
- 2 tbsp maple syrup

For the Filling:

- 1 cup mixed berries (strawberries, blueberries, raspberries)
- 1/4 cup coconut yogurt
- 1 tbsp maple syrup
- 1 tsp vanilla extract

DIRECTIONS

Prepare crust: Mix almond flour, melted coconut oil, and maple syrup. Press into a tart pan.
Bake: Preheat oven to 350°F (175°C). Bake for 10 minutes. Let cool.
Prepare filling: Mix coconut yogurt, maple syrup, and vanilla extract.
Assemble tart: Spread yogurt mixture over the cooled crust. Top with mixed berries.
Chill: Refrigerate for at least 1 hour.
Serve: Slice and serve.

Optional toppings: Garnish with mint leaves or a drizzle of additional maple syrup.

Per serving: 220 calories, 5g protein, 16g fats, 18g carbs

Chocolate Peanut Butter Pie

INGREDIENTS

Prep. time: 15 min   Cook time: 10 min   Serves: 4

For the Crust:

- 1 cup graham cracker crumbs
- 2 tbsp coconut oil, melted
- 2 tbsp maple syrup

For the Filling:

- 1/2 cup peanut butter
- 1/4 cup coconut cream (the thick part from a can of coconut milk)
- 1/4 cup maple syrup
- 1/2 cup dairy-free chocolate chips

DIRECTIONS

Prepare crust: Mix graham cracker crumbs, melted coconut oil, and maple syrup. Press into a pie pan.
Bake: Preheat oven to 350°F (175°C). Bake for 10 minutes. Let cool.
Prepare filling: In a bowl, mix peanut butter, coconut cream, and maple syrup until smooth. Melt chocolate chips in a microwave-safe bowl in 30-second intervals, stirring until smooth.
Assemble pie: Spread the peanut butter mixture over the cooled crust. Pour melted chocolate over the peanut butter layer, spreading it evenly.
Chill: Refrigerate for at least 2 hours until set.
Serve: Slice and serve.

Optional toppings: Garnish with chopped peanuts or a drizzle of extra melted chocolate.

Per serving: 380 calories, 8g protein, 24g fats, 30g carbs

Peach and Blueberry Galette

INGREDIENTS

Prep. time: 15 min   Cook time: 30 min   Serves: 4

For the Crust:

- 1 cup all-purpose flour
- 1/2 tsp salt
- 1/2 cup vegan butter, cold and cubed
- 2-4 tbsp ice water

For the Filling:

- 2 large peaches, sliced
- 1/2 cup blueberries
- 2 tbsp coconut sugar
- 1 tbsp cornstarch
- 1 tsp lemon juice

DIRECTIONS

Prepare crust: Mix flour and salt, cut in vegan butter until coarse crumbs form. Add ice water gradually until dough comes together. Chill for 30 minutes.
Prepare filling: Mix peaches, blueberries, coconut sugar, cornstarch, and lemon juice.
Assemble galette: Preheat oven to 375°F (190°C). Roll out dough on a floured surface, transfer to a baking sheet. Arrange fruit in the center, fold edges over.
Bake: Bake for 30-35 minutes until golden.
Cool and serve: Let cool for 10 minutes before serving.

Optional toppings: Serve with vegan vanilla ice cream or coconut whipped cream.

Per serving: 250 calories, 3g protein, 14g fats, 30g carbs

Avocado Chocolate Mousse

INGREDIENTS

Prep. time: 10 min   Cook time: 0 min   Serves: 4

- 2 ripe avocados
- 1/4 cup cocoa powder
- 1/4 cup maple syrup
- 1/4 cup almond milk
- 1 tsp vanilla extract
- Pinch of salt

DIRECTIONS

Blend ingredients: In a blender or food processor, combine avocados, cocoa powder, maple syrup, almond milk, vanilla extract, and a pinch of salt. Blend until smooth and creamy.
Chill: Transfer mousse to serving bowls and refrigerate for at least 30 minutes before serving.
Serve: Garnish with fresh berries, shredded coconut, or a sprinkle of cocoa powder.

Optional toppings: Add a dollop of coconut whipped cream or chopped nuts for extra flavor and texture.

Per serving: 180 calories, 3g protein, 14g fats, 20g carbs

Almond Flour Brownies

INGREDIENTS

Prep. time: 10 min   Cook time: 20 min   Serves: 4

- 1 cup almond flour
- 1/4 cup cocoa powder
- 1/2 cup coconut sugar
- 1/4 cup melted coconut oil
- 1/4 cup almond milk
- 1 tsp vanilla extract
- 1/2 tsp baking powder
- 1/4 tsp salt
- 1/4 cup dairy-free chocolate chips (optional)

DIRECTIONS

Preheat oven: Preheat to 350°F (175°C). Grease a small baking pan or line it with parchment paper.
Prepare batter: In a bowl, mix almond flour, cocoa powder, coconut sugar, baking powder, and salt. In another bowl, combine melted coconut oil, almond milk, and vanilla extract. Pour wet ingredients into dry ingredients and mix until just combined. Fold in chocolate chips if using.
Bake: Pour batter into the prepared pan and spread evenly. Bake for 18-20 minutes or until a toothpick inserted into the center comes out clean.
Cool: Let cool in the pan for 10 minutes, then transfer to a wire rack to cool completely.
Serve: Cut into squares and serve.

Optional toppings: Dust with powdered sugar or drizzle with melted chocolate.

Per serving: 250 calories, 5g protein, 18g fats, 20g carbs

Baked Apples with Cinnamon and Walnuts

INGREDIENTS

Prep. time: 10 min   Cook time: 30 min   Serves: 4

- 4 large apples, cored
- 1/4 cup walnuts, chopped
- 2 tbsp maple syrup
- 1 tsp ground cinnamon
- 1/4 tsp ground nutmeg
- 1/4 cup raisins (optional)
- 1 tbsp vegan butter, melted

DIRECTIONS

Preheat oven: Preheat to 350°F (175°C).
Prepare filling: In a bowl, mix chopped walnuts, maple syrup, cinnamon, nutmeg, and raisins if using.
Stuff apples: Place the cored apples in a baking dish. Stuff each apple with the walnut mixture. Drizzle melted vegan butter over the stuffed apples.
Bake: Bake for 25-30 minutes, or until the apples are tender.
Serve: Serve warm, optionally topped with a dollop of coconut whipped cream or a scoop of vegan vanilla ice cream.

Optional toppings: Garnish with a sprinkle of extra cinnamon or a drizzle of additional maple syrup.

Per serving: 180 calories, 2g protein, 8g fats, 28g carbs

Banana Nice Cream with Berries

INGREDIENTS

Prep. time: 5 min   Cook time: 0 min   Serves: 2

- 4 ripe bananas, sliced and frozen
- 1/2 tsp vanilla extract
- 2-3 tbsp almond milk (as needed for blending)
- 1/2 cup mixed berries (fresh or frozen)

DIRECTIONS

Prepare bananas: Slice ripe bananas and freeze them for at least 2 hours or overnight.
Blend ingredients: In a blender or food processor, combine frozen banana slices, vanilla extract, and almond milk. Blend until smooth and creamy, adding more almond milk as needed for blending.
Add berries: Add mixed berries and blend until just combined, leaving some berry pieces for texture.
Serve: Scoop into bowls and serve immediately.

Optional toppings: Top with extra fresh berries, chopped nuts, shredded coconut, or a drizzle of nut butter.

Per serving: 120 calories, 1g protein, 1g fats, 30g carbs

Strawberry Basil Sorbet

INGREDIENTS

Prep. time: 10 min   Cook time: 0 min   Serves: 2

- 2 cups fresh strawberries, hulled
- 1/4 cup fresh basil leaves
- 2 tbsp lemon juice
- 2-3 tbsp maple syrup (adjust to taste)
- 1/4 cup water

DIRECTIONS

Blend ingredients: In a blender or food processor, combine strawberries, basil leaves, lemon juice, maple syrup, and water. Blend until smooth.

Freeze mixture: Pour the mixture into a shallow dish and freeze for 2-3 hours, stirring every 30 minutes to break up ice crystals. Alternatively, use an ice cream maker according to the manufacturer's instructions.

Serve: Scoop into bowls and serve immediately.

Optional toppings: Garnish with fresh basil leaves or a few sliced strawberries.

Per serving: 90 calories, 1g protein, 0g fats, 22g carbs

Peanut Butter Banana Ice Cream Sandwiches

INGREDIENTS

Prep. time: 15 min   Cook time: 0 min   Serves: 4

For the Banana Ice Cream:

- 4 ripe bananas, sliced and frozen
- 1/2 tsp vanilla extract
- 2-3 tbsp almond milk (as needed for blending)

For the Sandwiches:

- 8 vegan cookies (store-bought or homemade)
- 1/4 cup peanut butter

DIRECTIONS

Prepare banana ice cream: In a blender or food processor, combine frozen banana slices, vanilla extract, and almond milk. Blend until smooth and creamy, adding more almond milk as needed for blending. Freeze for 1 hour to firm up.

Assemble sandwiches: Spread a layer of peanut butter on one side of each cookie. Scoop a generous amount of banana ice cream onto four of the cookies. Top with the remaining cookies, peanut butter side down, to form sandwiches.

Freeze sandwiches: Place the assembled sandwiches on a baking sheet and freeze for at least 1 hour, or until firm.

Serve: Enjoy immediately after removing from the freezer.

Optional toppings: Roll the edges of the sandwiches in chopped nuts, mini chocolate chips, or shredded coconut for extra texture and flavor.

Per serving: 250 calories, 6g protein, 12g fats, 34g carbs

Chapter 13: Beverages
Juices

Tropical Carrot Juice

INGREDIENTS

Prep. time: 10 min   Cook time: 0 min   Serves: 2

- 4 large carrots, peeled and chopped
- 1 cup pineapple chunks (fresh or canned)
- 1 orange, peeled and segmented
- 1/2 inch piece of ginger, peeled
- 1/2 cup coconut water
- 1 tbsp lemon juice

DIRECTIONS

Blend ingredients: In a blender or juicer, combine carrots, pineapple chunks, orange segments, ginger, coconut water, and lemon juice. Blend until smooth.
Strain juice: Pour the mixture through a fine mesh strainer or cheesecloth into a pitcher to remove the pulp, if desired.
Serve: Pour into glasses and serve immediately.

Optional toppings: Garnish with a slice of pineapple or a sprig of mint.

Per serving: 120 calories, 2g protein, 1g fats, 28g carbs

Green Detox Juice

INGREDIENTS

Prep. time: 10 min   Cook time: 0 min   Serves: 2

- 1 cucumber, chopped
- 2 celery stalks, chopped
- 1 green apple, cored and chopped
- 1 cup spinach leaves
- 1/2 lemon, peeled
- 1-inch piece of ginger, peeled
- 1/2 cup water

DIRECTIONS

Blend ingredients: In a blender or juicer, combine cucumber, celery, green apple, spinach, lemon, ginger, and water. Blend until smooth.
Strain juice: Pour the mixture through a fine mesh strainer or cheesecloth into a pitcher to remove the pulp, if desired.
Serve: Pour into glasses and serve immediately.

Optional toppings: Garnish with a slice of lemon or a sprig of mint.

Per serving: 70 calories, 1g protein, 0g fats, 18g carbs

Berry Blast Juice

INGREDIENTS

Prep. time: 10 min   Cook time: 0 min   Serves: 2

- 1 cup strawberries, hulled
- 1 cup blueberries
- 1 cup raspberries
- 1 apple, cored and chopped
- 1/2 lemon, peeled
- 1/2 cup water

DIRECTIONS

Instructions: Blend ingredients: In a blender or juicer, combine strawberries, blueberries, raspberries, apple, lemon, and water. Blend until smooth.

Strain juice: Pour the mixture through a fine mesh strainer or cheesecloth into a pitcher to remove the pulp, if desired.

Serve: Pour into glasses and serve immediately.

Optional toppings: Garnish with a few whole berries or a sprig of mint.

Per serving: 100 calories, 1g protein, 0g fats, 25g carbs

Apple Celery Cleanser

INGREDIENTS

Prep. time: 10 min   Cook time: 0 min   Serves: 2

- 2 apples, cored and chopped
- 3 celery stalks, chopped
- 1 cucumber, chopped
- 1/2 lemon, peeled
- 1-inch piece of ginger, peeled
- 1/2 cup water

DIRECTIONS

Blend ingredients: In a blender or juicer, combine apples, celery, cucumber, lemon, ginger, and water. Blend until smooth.

Strain juice: Pour the mixture through a fine mesh strainer or cheesecloth into a pitcher to remove the pulp, if desired.

Serve: Pour into glasses and serve immediately.

Optional toppings: Garnish with a slice of apple or a celery stalk.

Per serving: 80 calories, 1g protein, 0g fats, 20g carbs

Mango Orange Sunrise

INGREDIENTS

Prep. time: 10 min   Cook time: 0 min   Serves: 2

- 1 large mango, peeled and chopped
- 2 oranges, peeled and segmented
- 1/2 cup pineapple chunks (fresh or canned)
- 1/2 inch piece of ginger, peeled
- 1/4 cup coconut water

DIRECTIONS

Blend ingredients: In a blender, combine mango, oranges, pineapple chunks, ginger, and coconut water. Blend until smooth.

Strain juice: Pour the mixture through a fine mesh strainer or cheesecloth into a pitcher to remove the pulp, if desired.

Serve: Pour into glasses and serve immediately.

Optional toppings: Garnish with a slice of orange or a sprig of mint.

Per serving: 120 calories, 2g protein, 1g fats, 30g carbs

Beetroot and Apple Juice

INGREDIENTS

Prep. time: 10 min   Cook time: 0 min   Serves: 2

- 2 medium beetroots, peeled and chopped
- 2 apples, cored and chopped
- 1 carrot, peeled and chopped
- 1/2 lemon, peeled
- 1-inch piece of ginger, peeled
- 1/2 cup water

DIRECTIONS

Blend ingredients: In a blender or juicer, combine beetroots, apples, carrot, lemon, ginger, and water. Blend until smooth.

Strain juice: Pour the mixture through a fine mesh strainer or cheesecloth into a pitcher to remove the pulp, if desired.

Serve: Pour into glasses and serve immediately.

Optional toppings: Garnish with a slice of lemon or a few mint leaves.

Per serving: 110 calories, 2g protein, 0g fats, 26g carbs

Plant-Based Milks

Almond milk

INGREDIENTS

Prep. time: 10 min   Cook time: 0 min   Serves: 2

- 1 cup raw almonds
- 3 cups water (for blending)
- 1-2 tbsp maple syrup (optional, for sweetness)
- 1 tsp vanilla extract (optional)
- Pinch of salt

DIRECTIONS

Soak almonds: Soak almonds in water for at least 8 hours or overnight. Drain and rinse.

Blend ingredients: In a blender, combine soaked almonds, 3 cups of water, maple syrup (if using), vanilla extract (if using), and a pinch of salt. Blend until smooth and creamy.

Strain milk: Pour the mixture through a nut milk bag or cheesecloth into a pitcher to remove the almond pulp. Squeeze well to extract all the liquid.

Serve: Pour into glasses and serve immediately or store in the refrigerator for up to 3 days.

Optional toppings: Add a sprinkle of cinnamon or a dash of cocoa powder for extra flavor.

Per serving: 70 calories, 2g protein, 4g fats, 8g carbs

Vanilla Cashew Milk

INGREDIENTS

Prep. time: 10 min   Cook time: 0 min   Serves: 2

- 1 cup raw cashews
- 3 cups water (for blending)
- 1-2 tbsp maple syrup (optional, for sweetness)
- 1 tsp vanilla extract
- Pinch of salt

DIRECTIONS

Soak cashews: Soak cashews in water for at least 4 hours or overnight. Drain and rinse.

Blend ingredients: In a blender, combine soaked cashews, 3 cups of water, maple syrup (if using), vanilla extract, and a pinch of salt. Blend until smooth and creamy.

Strain milk (optional): If a smoother texture is desired, pour the mixture through a nut milk bag or cheesecloth into a pitcher.

Serve: Pour into glasses and serve immediately or store in the refrigerator for up to 3 days.

Optional toppings: Add a sprinkle of cinnamon or a dash of nutmeg for extra flavor.

Per serving: 90 calories, 3g protein, 6g fats, 8g carbs

Plant-Based Milks

Hazelnut Milk

INGREDIENTS

Prep. time: 10 min   Cook time: 0 min   Serves: 2

- 1 cup raw hazelnuts
- 3 cups water (for blending)
- 1-2 tbsp maple syrup (optional, for sweetness)
- 1 tsp vanilla extract (optional)
- Pinch of salt

DIRECTIONS

Soak hazelnuts: Soak hazelnuts in water for at least 8 hours or overnight. Drain and rinse.

Blend ingredients: In a blender, combine soaked hazelnuts, 3 cups of water, maple syrup (if using), vanilla extract (if using), and a pinch of salt. Blend until smooth and creamy.

Strain milk: Pour the mixture through a nut milk bag or cheesecloth into a pitcher to remove the hazelnut pulp. Squeeze well to extract all the liquid.

Serve: Pour into glasses and serve immediately or store in the refrigerator for up to 3 days.

Optional toppings: Add a sprinkle of cocoa powder or a dash of cinnamon for extra flavor.

Per serving: 100 calories, 2g protein, 8g fats, 4g carbs

Rich Coconut Milk

INGREDIENTS

Prep. time: 10 min   Cook time: 0 min   Serves: 2

- 1 cup shredded unsweetened coconut
- 2 cups hot water
- 1-2 tbsp maple syrup (optional, for sweetness)
- 1 tsp vanilla extract (optional)
- Pinch of salt

DIRECTIONS

Blend ingredients: In a blender, combine shredded coconut and hot water. Blend on high for 2-3 minutes until smooth and creamy.

Strain milk: Pour the mixture through a nut milk bag or cheesecloth into a pitcher to remove the coconut pulp. Squeeze well to extract all the liquid.

Add flavor: If desired, mix in maple syrup, vanilla extract, and a pinch of salt.

Serve: Pour into glasses and serve immediately or store in the refrigerator for up to 3 days.

Optional toppings: Add a sprinkle of cinnamon or a dash of nutmeg for extra flavor.

Per serving: 150 calories, 1g protein, 15g fats, 4g carbs

Plant-Based Milks

Oat Milk

INGREDIENTS

Prep. time: 10 min   Cook time: 0 min   Serves: 2

- 1 cup rolled oats
- 3 cups water (for blending)
- 1-2 tbsp maple syrup (optional, for sweetness)
- 1 tsp vanilla extract (optional)
- Pinch of salt

DIRECTIONS

Rinse oats: Rinse rolled oats under cold water to remove any excess starch.

Blend ingredients: In a blender, combine rinsed oats, 3 cups of water, maple syrup (if using), vanilla extract (if using), and a pinch of salt. Blend on high for 30-45 seconds until smooth.

Strain milk: Pour the mixture through a nut milk bag or cheesecloth into a pitcher to remove the oat pulp. Squeeze well to extract all the liquid.

Serve: Pour into glasses and serve immediately or store in the refrigerator for up to 3 days.

Optional toppings: Add a sprinkle of cinnamon or a dash of nutmeg for extra flavor.

Per serving: 90 calories, 3g protein, 1.5g fats, 18g carbs

Sunflower Seed Milk

INGREDIENTS

Prep. time: 10 min   Cook time: 0 min   Serves: 2

- 1 cup raw sunflower seeds
- 3 cups water (for blending)
- 1-2 tbsp maple syrup (optional, for sweetness)
- 1 tsp vanilla extract (optional)
- Pinch of salt

DIRECTIONS

Soak sunflower seeds: Soak sunflower seeds in water for at least 4 hours or overnight. Drain and rinse.

Blend ingredients: In a blender, combine soaked sunflower seeds, 3 cups of water, maple syrup (if using), vanilla extract (if using), and a pinch of salt. Blend until smooth and creamy.

Strain milk: Pour the mixture through a nut milk bag or cheesecloth into a pitcher to remove the sunflower seed pulp. Squeeze well to extract all the liquid.

Serve: Pour into glasses and serve immediately or store in the refrigerator for up to 3 days.

Optional toppings: Add a sprinkle of cinnamon or a dash of cocoa powder for extra flavor.

Per serving: 110 calories, 4g protein, 9g fats, 5g carbs

Calming Chamomile Lavender Tea

INGREDIENTS

Prep. time: 5 min   Cook time: 5 min   Serves: 2

- 2 cups water
- 2 tbsp dried chamomile flowers
- 1 tsp dried lavender flowers
- 1-2 tsp honey or maple syrup (optional, for sweetness)
- Lemon slices (optional, for garnish)

DIRECTIONS

Boil water: Bring 2 cups of water to a boil in a small pot.
Add herbs: Remove from heat and add chamomile and lavender flowers.
Steep: Cover and let steep for 5 minutes.
Strain: Strain the tea into cups to remove the flowers.
Serve: Add honey or maple syrup if desired. Garnish with lemon slices.

Optional toppings: Add a sprinkle of cinnamon or a few fresh mint leaves for extra flavor.

Per serving: 5 calories, 0g protein, 0g fats, 1g carbs

Refreshing Mint and Lemon Balm Infusion

INGREDIENTS

Prep. time: 5 min   Cook time: 5 min   Serves: 2

- 2 cups water
- 2 tbsp fresh mint leaves (or 1 tbsp dried mint)
- 2 tbsp fresh lemon balm leaves (or 1 tbsp dried lemon balm)
- 1-2 tsp honey or maple syrup (optional, for sweetness)
- Lemon slices (optional, for garnish)

DIRECTIONS

Boil water: Bring 2 cups of water to a boil in a small pot.
Add herbs: Remove from heat and add mint and lemon balm leaves.
Steep: Cover and let steep for 5 minutes.
Strain: Strain the infusion into cups to remove the leaves.
Serve: Add honey or maple syrup if desired. Garnish with lemon slices.

Optional toppings: Add a few fresh mint leaves or a slice of lemon for extra flavor.

Per serving: 5 calories, 0g protein, 0g fats, 1g carbs

Citrus Rooibos Infusion

INGREDIENTS

Prep. time: 5 min   Cook time: 5 min   Serves: 2

- 2 cups water
- 2 tbsp rooibos tea leaves
- 1 orange, sliced
- 1 lemon, sliced
- 1-2 tsp honey or maple syrup (optional, for sweetness)

DIRECTIONS

Boil water: Bring 2 cups of water to a boil in a small pot.
Add rooibos and citrus: Remove from heat and add rooibos tea leaves, orange slices, and lemon slices.
Steep: Cover and let steep for 5 minutes.
Strain: Strain the infusion into cups to remove the tea leaves and fruit slices.
Serve: Add honey or maple syrup if desired.

Optional toppings: Garnish with a fresh orange or lemon slice.

Per serving: 10 calories, 0g protein, 0g fats, 3g carbs

Detoxifying Dandelion Root Tea

INGREDIENTS

Prep. time: 5 min   Cook time: 10 min   Serves: 2

DIRECTIONS

- 2 cups water
- 2 tbsp dried dandelion root
- 1-2 tsp honey or maple syrup (optional, for sweetness)
- Lemon slices (optional, for garnish)

Boil water: Bring 2 cups of water to a boil in a small pot.
Add dandelion root: Reduce heat, add dried dandelion root, and simmer for 10 minutes.
Strain: Strain the tea into cups to remove the dandelion root.
Serve: Add honey or maple syrup if desired. Garnish with lemon slices.

Optional toppings: Add a sprinkle of cinnamon or a fresh mint leaf for extra flavor.

Per serving: 5 calories, 0g protein, 0g fats, 1g carbs

Teas and Infusions

Spicy Ginger Turmeric Tea

INGREDIENTS

Prep. time: 5 min   Cook time: 10 min   Serves: 2

- 2 cups water
- 1-inch piece fresh ginger, peeled and sliced
- 1 tsp ground turmeric (or 1-inch piece fresh turmeric, sliced)
- 1/4 tsp ground black pepper
- 1-2 tbsp lemon juice
- 1-2 tsp honey or maple syrup (optional, for sweetness)
- Lemon slices (optional, for garnish)

DIRECTIONS

Boil water: Bring 2 cups of water to a boil in a small pot.
Add ginger and turmeric: Reduce heat and add ginger slices, turmeric, and black pepper.
Simmer: Let simmer for 10 minutes.
Strain: Strain the tea into cups to remove the ginger and turmeric pieces.
Serve: Add lemon juice and honey or maple syrup if desired. Garnish with lemon slices.

Optional toppings: Add a sprinkle of cayenne pepper for extra spice.

Per serving: 10 calories, 0g protein, 0g fats, 3g carbs

Soothing Rosehip and Hibiscus Tea

INGREDIENTS

Prep. time: 5 min   Cook time: 10 min   Serves: 2

DIRECTIONS

- 2 cups water
- 2 tbsp dried rosehips
- 2 tbsp dried hibiscus flowers
- 1-2 tsp honey or maple syrup (optional, for sweetness)
- Lemon slices (optional, for garnish)

Boil water: Bring 2 cups of water to a boil in a small pot.
Add herbs: Remove from heat and add dried rosehips and hibiscus flowers.
Steep: Cover and let steep for 10 minutes.
Strain: Strain the tea into cups to remove the flowers.
Serve: Add honey or maple syrup if desired. Garnish with lemon slices.

Optional toppings: Add a few fresh mint leaves for extra flavor.

Per serving: 5 calories, 0g protein, 0g fats, 1g carbs

Chapter 14: Kitchen Conversion Chart

Dry Weights

1/2 oz = 1 tbsp = 1/16 cup = 15 g

1 oz = 2 tbsp = 1/8 cup = 28 g

2 oz = 4 tbsp = 1/4 cup = 57 g

4 oz = 8 tbsp = 1/2 cup = 115 g

8 oz = 16 tbsp = 1 cup = 227 g

12 oz = 24 tbsp = 1 1/2 cups = 340 g

16 oz = 32 tbsp = 2 cups = 455 g

Liquid Volumes

1 oz = 2 tbsp = 1/8 cup = 30 ml

2 oz = 4 tbsp = 1/4 cup = 60 ml

4 oz = 8 tbsp = 1/2 cup = 120 ml

8 oz = 16 tbsp = 1 cup = 237 ml

12 oz = 24 tbsp = 1 1/2 cups = 355 ml

16 oz = 32 tbsp = 2 cups = 473 ml

32 oz = 64 tbsp = 4 cups = 946 ml

Baking Pan

9-inch (by 3") standard round pan = 12 cups

9-inch (by 2.5") springform pan = 10 cups

10-inch (by 4") tube pan = 16 cups

10-inch (by 3") bundt pan = 12 cups

9-inch (by 13") rectangular pan = 12 cups

8-inch (by 8") square pan = 8 cups

9 x 5-inch loaf pan = 8 cups

General Conversions

1 oz = 28 grams

1 lb = 454 grams

1 cup = 227 grams

1 tsp = 5 ml

1 tbsp = 15 ml

1 oz = 30 ml

1 cup = 237 ml

1 pint = 473 ml (2 cups)

1 gallon = 16 cups

Abbreviations

tbsp = Tablespoon

tsp = Teaspoon

fl.oz. = Fluid Ounce

c = cup

ml = Milliliter

lb = pound

F = Fahrenheit

° = Celsius

ml = Milliliter

g = grams

kg = kilograms

l = liter

Oven Temperature

150°C = 250°F

165°C = 325°F

180°C = 350°F

190°C = 375°F

200°C = 400°F

220°C = 425°F

Chapter 15: 28-Day Meal Plan

1-7 Day Meal Plan

Day	Breakfast	Lunch	Snacks	Dinner
Day-1	Berry Bliss Smoothie Bowl (280 calories) p19	Curried Cauliflower and Potato Stew (300 calories) p58	Crispy Baked Chickpea Snacks (180 calories) p33	Spaghetti with Lentil Bolognese (350 calories) p59
Day-2	Fluffy Vegan Blueberry Pancakes (300 calories) p28	Silky Butternut Squash Soup (300 calories) p52	Coconut Cashew Energy Balls (250 calories) p34	Mushroom and Wild Rice Casserole (300 calories) p63
Day-3	Green Goddess Smoothie (220 calories) p19	Peanut Sauce Noodles with Tofu (350 calories) p59	Mixed Greens with Avocado and Citrus Vinaigrette (220 calories) p42	Caramelized Onion and Arugula Pizza (300 calories) p72
Day-4	Sesame Porridge with Lemon (320 calories) p24	Creamy Potato Gratin (300 calories) p62	Baked Apples with Cinnamon and Walnuts (180 calories) p89	Coconut Curry Chickpeas (300 calories) p76
Day-5	Classic Avocado Toast (300 calories) p25	Mushroom and Spinach White Pizza (320 calories) p71	Almond Coconut Protein Bars (300 calories) p35	Grilled Veggie and Hummus Wraps (250 calories) p65
Day-6	Berry Burst Overnight Oats (310 calories) p22	Quinoa and Roasted Veggie Tacos (350 calories) p66	Fresh Veggie Spring Rolls (150 calories) p36	Millet and Edamame Salad with Ginger Lime Dressing (300 calories) p46
Day-7	Flaxseed Porridge with Banana (350 calories) p24	Black Bean and Sweet Potato Burgers (350 calories) p68	Garlic Roasted Brussels Sprouts (150 calories) p73	Bulgur Wheat and Kidney Bean Herb Salad (250 calories) p47

8-14 Day Meal Plan

Day	Breakfast	Lunch	Snacks	Dinner
Day-8	Vanilla Chia Seed Pancakes (320 calories) p28	Thai Peanut Tofu Wraps (400 calories) p66	Almond Butter Oatmeal Bars (250 calories) p79	Creamy Coconut Lentil Dal (320 calories) p78
Day-9	Banana Oatmeal Breakfast Smoothie (330 calories) p21	Mushroom and Barley Stew (300 calories) p55	Savory Kale Chips (120 calories) p33	Couscous and Red Bean Salad with Mint and Parsley (300 calories) p45
Day-10	Mushroom and Spinach Tofu Scramble (250 calories) p25	Classic Vegetable Lasagna (400 calories) p62	Berry Nutty Snack Mix (280 calories) p35	Quinoa and Kale Stew (250 calories) p57
Day-11	Tropical Sunrise Smoothie Bowl (350 calories) p20	Pasta Primavera with Cashew Cream Sauce (350 calories) p60	Classic Caesar Salad with Vegan Parmesan (220 calories) p41	Classic Tomato Basil Soup (150 calories) p51
Day-12	Tropical Fruit and Nut Granola (350 calories) p32	Creamy Coconut Carrot Soup (250 calories) p51	Pumpkin Spice Energy Balls (210 calories) p34	Spiced Lentil and Rice Pilaf (280 calories) p77
Day-13	Crispy Almond Flour Waffles (320 calories) p30	Vegan Pesto Pasta with Cherry Tomatoes (350 calories) p61	Roasted Garlic Mushrooms (120 calories) p75	Kale and Quinoa Salad with Lemon Tahini Dressing (280 calories) p44
Day-14	Banana Cinnamon Apple Pie Overnight Oats (320 calories) p22	Grilled Veggie and Pesto Paninis (350 calories) p69	Spring Mix Salad with Roasted Beets and Orange Segments (180 calories) p43	Lentil and Root Vegetable Stew (300 calories) p56

15-21 Day Meal Plan

Day	Breakfast	Lunch	Snacks	Dinner
Day-15	Savory Chickpea Flour Waffles (250 calories) p30	Mushroom and Spinach White Pizza (320 calories) p71	Crispy Parmesan Cauliflower (180 calories) p75	Spicy Lentil Tacos (250 calories) p65
Day-16	Beetroot Detox Smoothie (180 calories) p20	Chickpea Shawarma Wraps (350 calories) p67	Spinach and Strawberry Salad with Poppy Seed Dressing (200 calories) p41	Spicy Sesame Soba Noodles (300 calories) p61
Day-17	Blueberry Almond Amaranth Porridge (360 calories) p27	Simple Minestrone Soup (250 calories) p54	Lemon Coconut Bliss Bars (210 calories) p81	Quinoa and Black Bean Salad with Avocado Dressing (350 calories) p45
Day-18	Peanut Butter Banana Chia Pudding (320 calories) p23	Chunky Vegetable and Bean Stew (250 calories) p55	Sweet Potato and Avocado Bites (250 calories) p37	Ginger Miso Soup with Tofu (150 calories) p52
Day-19	Tropical Sunrise Smoothie Bowl (350 calories) p20	Peanut Sauce Noodles with Tofu (350 calories) p59	Balsamic Glazed Carrots (120 calories) p74	Savory Tofu and Cabbage Stew (250 calories) p58
Day-20	Burrito with Black Beans (350 calories) p26	Sweet Potato and Kale Gratin (280 calories) p64	Banana Nice Cream with Berries (120 calories) p89	Brown Rice and Lentil Salad with Lemon Vinaigrette (320 calories) p44
Day-21	Banana Tofu Pancakes (340 calories) p29	Curried Sweet Potato Soup (300 calories) p53	Cucumber and Mint Salad with Lime Dressing (120 calories) p43	Classic Veggie Burger with Avocado (350 calories) p70

22-28 Day Meal Plan

Day	Breakfast	Lunch	Snacks	Dinner
Day-22	Chickpea & Avocado Breakfast Toast (350 calories) p26	Quinoa and Beet Burgers (320 calories) p68	Crispy Cauliflower Bites (160 calories) p37	Barley and White Bean Salad with Pesto (180 calories) p46
Day-23	Warm Cinnamon Quinoa Porridge (350 calories) p27	Mexican Black Bean and Corn Bake (250 calories) p64	Avocado Chocolate Mousse (180 calories) p88	Sweet Potato and Black Bean Stew (300 calories) p76
Day-24	Chocolate Almond Butter Smoothie Bowl (350 calories) p21	Lemon Chickpea Orzo Soup (250 calories) p53	Lemon Herb Quinoa Pilaf (180 calories) p76	Chickpea Salad Sandwiches (320 calories) p69
Day-25	Mushroom and Spinach Tofu Scramble (250 calories) p25	Lemon Garlic Pasta with Asparagus (300 calories) p60	Rosemary Sweet Potato Wedges (220 calories) p73	Herbed Chickpea and Tomato Salad (220 calories) p47
Day-26	Blueberry Lemon Chia Pudding (250 calories) p23	Mediterranean Veggie Sandwich (300 calories) p70	No-Bake Chocolate Peanut Butter Bars (250 calories) p81	Black Bean and Avocado Tacos (220 calories) p67
Day-27	Chocolate Chip Oatmeal Pancakes (350 calories) p29	Hearty Chickpea and Spinach Stew (220 calories) p56	Arugula and Pear Salad with Walnuts and Balsamic Glaze (220 calories) p42	Green Pea and Mint Soup (200 calories) p54
Day-28	Crunchy Almond Maple Granola (300 calories) p32	Pineapple and Tempeh Hawaiian Pizza (320 calories) p72	Maple Roasted Butternut Squash (200 calories) p74	Butternut Squash and Spinach Casserole (250 calories) p63

Conclusion

As we conclude our culinary journey through the vibrant world of plant-based eating, I hope this cookbook has inspired you to embrace the rich and nourishing possibilities that plant-based cuisine offers. The recipes and tips shared here are more than just a collection of meals; they represent steps toward a healthier, more sustainable, and compassionate lifestyle.

Transitioning to a plant-based diet is not merely about changing what's on your plate—it's about cultivating a deeper connection with the food we consume, understanding its profound impact on our health, and the environment, and aligning our choices with our values. Whether your motivation stems from health considerations, ethical beliefs, or environmental concerns, a plant-based diet provides a fulfilling pathway to achieving these goals while enjoying delicious and satisfying meals.

This book has been crafted with accessibility in mind, offering a diverse range of recipes that are flavorful, nutritious, and easy to prepare. It aims to make plant-based living approachable, whether you're just beginning your journey or have been cooking plant-based meals for years. From hearty breakfasts to indulgent desserts, each recipe celebrates the goodness of natural, whole foods that nourish both you and the planet.

As you continue on your plant-based journey, remember that every small change contributes to a larger positive impact. Be adventurous, try new ingredients, and savor the process of discovering new flavors and textures. The exploration of plant-based eating is an ongoing adventure of creativity and taste, with endless possibilities awaiting your discovery.

Thank you for allowing me to share these recipes and insights with you. I hope this cookbook has been a valuable resource and a wellspring of inspiration. Here's to a future filled with delicious plant-based meals, vibrant health, and a more sustainable, compassionate world. May you enjoy every step and every bite of your plant-based journey, and may it bring you joy, health, and fulfillment.

Made in United States
Troutdale, OR
11/01/2024

24362167R00060